The Irish Cookbook

by

Carla Blake

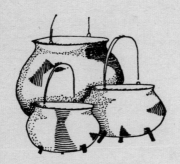

THE MERCIER ·PRESS
DUBLIN and CORK

Acknowledgements

I should like to thank my husband for all his help, Margot Tucker and Maeve Curtis for their many excellent suggestions, and my daughters: Rosalie for her illustrations, and Claire for her help in testing these recipes. I also appreciate the advice given on metrication by Mrs Johanna Senior of the Women's Advisory Committee British Standards Institution; and all the assistance given by Countess Karin von der Schulenburg.

Preface

The Irish Cookbook is Carla Blake's first cookbook and one hopes it won't be her last. It was born of a burning desire to pass on to others what pleasure can be got out of cooking for the family.

Reading through the contents one senses that reverence for food and cooking, more often attributed to the French cook.

The author has the rare gift of turning the simplest meal into a festive one – flavourful and colourful and involving the minimum of utensils and effort.

Every recipe in the book, the author claims, is tried and trusted and they're not just lists of ingredients followed by a trite description of how the dish is put together. They're a warm hearted treatise on ways of dealing with food with little asides on her own personal likes and fancies, and though it is in the main a practical, down-to-earth recipe book on Irish food and Irish cooking, expensive items such as fresh salmon, shell fish, and the uncommon vegetables such as artichokes, asparagus and celeriac are also included.

In addition to being of enormous help to any housewife in search of a reliable textbook of Irish food and home cooking *The Irish Cookbook* should be of value to farm guesthouse keepers, who, all over the country, are making a name for themselves as being an important part of the tourist industry.

I will buy the book to send to my numerous friends abroad who want to know more about Irish cooking.

Wisely, the author has converted her recipes into metrication. In a few years time the recipe book which hasn't made this conversion will be somewhat out of date.

Whether you are looking for soups or sauces, cheese dip or curried chicken, herrings or hors d'oeuvre, barm brack or boiled ham, drisheen or roast duckling, mackerel or mayonnaise, you'll find each recipe set out with meticulous care, easy to follow, and, where possible, fresh from garden, orchard, river, sea or lake, or local butcher.

I recommend this earnest cook book as a valuable addition to the kitchen book shelf. For the young housewife it could be the start of a collection.

MAEVE CURTIS

Contents

Potato Dishes – Soda Bread – Barm Brack – Porter
Cake and Pudding – Carrageen

A Drinks Party – Beer Party – Buffet or Fork
Suppers for Twenty, including Teenage Party, and an
Inexpensive Fork Supper – Elegant Little Dinner
Parties – Ideas for a Child's Party – Cakes for
Morning Coffee

Important

The apparent discrepancies in converting avoirdupois to metric
measures in this book are because in recipes where the proportions
do not have to be exact I have used the most convenient amounts.
For instance, one would not buy 672 g of meat or fish which is
exactly equivalent to 1½ lb, but would ask for 750 g or ¾ kg. The
difference in total quantities is 84 g, under 3 oz, which is a trivial
amount. See also the information on metrication on p. 12.

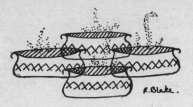

Foreword

When I got married I could not cook at all, I learned the hard way, literally 'slaving over a hot stove' until I profited from my mistakes and gradually came to enjoy cooking – and the results of my labours. What I needed in these first few months was a cookery book simple enough for a beginner, which gave guidance on how to plan meals for balance in colour, taste and texture as well as food value. I wanted to be told that roast beef needs Yorkshire pudding, that lamb and mint sauce go together like strawberries and cream, what sauces bring out the best in fish and vegetables.

That is what this book is about: ideas for good combinations of food, my pet short cuts and economies, dishes pleasing alike to eye, nose and palate. There is a section on 'Quick and Easy' recipes, for when things pile up on you, or the baby cries all morning and needs 'cosying'. There are some 'money savers' for the times when funds are low, or you suddenly feel that the family has been 'living too high off the pig's back'. Also there are some ideas for entertaining, when one wants something unusual. All the ingredients are obtainable in a country town like Fermoy.

This is really a 'common place book' such as our grandmothers kept, a collection of recipes which I, ordinary wife and mother, have found useful for all occasions. Some are my own invention, some use piquant mixtures, most of them are just plain delicious and the family has eaten up and 'asked for more'.

I have tried in most cases to give all the steps in the preparation of each dish, this may lead to a certain amount of repetition but these pages will keep cleaner and your temper less
frayed if there are few cross references. Included are a selection
of modern Irish recipes and many traditional Irish dishes,
though for centuries life was hard and the people were thankful
for potatoes (or poppies), skim milk, and a little 'American' fat
bacon.

In Ireland we have an abundance of gorgeous natural produce such as creamy milk, 'the very best butter', floury potatoes
and crispy fresh vegetables; fish of every sort, and the most
succulent meat, ham and bacon. On the whole it is best to use
fresh foods in season; although the present wide choice of tinned, dehydrated and frozen products enlarges our range, they
tend to be comparatively expensive and less distinctive in flavour. Herbs and spices, and delicatessen supplies like liver
sausage, cream cheese and new sauces add infinite variety to
our meals.

Planning is important. Follow a smooth bland concoction
like macaroni cheese with something that has bite and flavour,
for instance ham and a crisp salad of celery, diced apple and
beetroot. Prawns tossed in butter, served on a small square of
very crunchy fried bread are a good contrast to pork steaks
with mushrooms in cream sauce, or tender roast lamb. A cream
soup before a creamy second course (fish with white sauce) or
tomato soup when the meal includes grilled tomatoes are dull.

Have you ever wondered how the colours of the Irish flag
came to be chosen? I like to believe they were inspired by the
glory of our countryside in Spring: the tender young green of
growing things, the fragile thorn blossom foaming white in the
hedges, and the golden beauty of honey-scented gorse; life and
hope after a long Winter.

I once planned a St Patrick's Day dinner party on this colour
scheme; each course was green, white and gold. Naturally we
started with traditional Irish potato soup, aromatic with herbs,
and added golden fried bread cubes at table; then poached eggs
on spinach with Hollandaise sauce; followed by succulent Irish
ham and salad St Patrick: lettuce, sliced orange, diced celery
and apple, with a rich yellow mayonnaise. To finish we had hot

lemon meringue pie on an emerald green plate. China and table mats toned in, and the flowers were golden daffodils in a Waterford glass bowl. Alas, I did not rise to Irish coffee as a grand finale. Simple though the instructions sound, it is most difficult to make it scalding hot at home, and it is better left to those deft experts with little spirit lamps who produce it like magicians when one dines out in style.

Given a bright airy kitchen, which is after all the heart of our home, with the basic necessities of an efficient cooker, refrigerator, hot water and washing machine, I consider an electric hand mixer and a small blender the most valuable extra acquisitions.

Another absolutely essential labour saving device is – wait for it – *help from the family*. Insist that the children take turns in washing up (yes, the boys too!) and should Himself offer a hand with the dishes accept with alacrity and appreciation. Encourage the small fry to take an interest in cooking, and let them try their hand at it, just think how grateful your future sons- and daughters-in-law will be. Give yourself some free time by planning ahead, cook double quantities of potatoes or rice sometimes, or casserole dishes for reheating next day.

In spite of all the talk now-a-days for how dreary a woman's life is, tied to the chores and the children, there is still great joy and fulfilment in turning a house into a home, where the family want to spend their time and friends are welcome. If I do occasionally feel rather fed up at the thought of producing yet another meal, I smugly remind myself that, as Owen Meredith said:

'We may live without poetry, music and art;
We may live without conscience and live without heart;
We may live without friends, we may live without books,
But civilized man cannot live without cooks'.

Useful Things to Know

Metrication

Ingredients throughout the book are given in both metric and avoirdupois measures. It is awkward and unsatisfactory to convert pounds directly to kilos or the other way about, therefore the Womens' Advisory Council of the British Standards Institution has decided to base recipes on the 25 gramme (25 g) unit as the most convenient equivalent to 1 oz. Wherever possible I have followed this system, rounding off amounts where quantities need not be absolutely accurate; this explains any apparent discrepancies in conversion. For larger amounts of meat or vegetables I have roughly equated 1 kilo (1 kg) to 2 lb., i.e. 500 g to 1 lb and cooking times are based on this. Where the balance of the ingredients has to be exact, as for cheese soufflé or puff pastry, etc. I have equalled 28 g to 1 oz.

For liquid measures 1 litre (1 l) is approximately 1¾ pints, and I am using the equivalents of 600 millilitres (600 ml) to 1 pint, as metric measuring jugs will be marked in 100 ml divisions.

Measures

When measures are given in tablespoons, dessertspoons or teaspoons, this indicates level spoonfuls unless otherwise stated. The cup used for measuring is an average breakfast cup which holds 300 ml (½ pint).

Butter

Butter is used as an ingredient in most of the recipes. It is such an easy way of improving the taste, texture and aroma of anything from soup to savoury that I would economize on most other things before I would consider giving up using it! I use margarine in cakes and some pastry.

Cream

Cream adds a gorgeous richness and smoothness, be as lavish as you can with it – carefully skimmed top milk is better than no cream.

Oven Temperatures

These are given as a guide to the heat required – for instance a moderately hot oven (205°C gas mark 6) may be anything from 200°C to 210°C, the temperature is approximate. Oven temperatures differ with the type of cooker, usually the appropriate settings will be given in the manufacturers instruction book.

Oven	Gasmark	Centigrade	Fahrenheit
cool oven	½	5°C	270°F
very low oven	1–2	145°–155°C	290°–310°F
low oven	3	170°C	335°F
very moderate	4	180°C	355°F
moderate	5	195°C	380°F
moderately hot	6	205°C	400°F
hot	7	220°C	425°F
very hot	8–9	230°–250°C	445°–480°F

This is an approximale guide, as cookers vary greatly.

Cooking Times

Cooking times are to be used as a general guide, but as ovens differ learn to know your oven, and note whether it is quicker or slower than the given times.

Soup

Most people like soup: thick and flavoursome, and full of 'bits' if a light meal is to follow; or clear and appetizing to give zest to a rich second course. Cream soups are warming and filling and also make a good winter supper dish with crispy fried bread cubes, or a handful of grated cheese or rashers fried till crisp and then broken into small pieces. As we say in Ireland 'There's both eating and drinking in it!'

Allow 200 ml ($\frac{1}{3}$ pint) for each person. Soup stays hotter if served in soup cups. There are many good packet and tinned soups on the market now, which are not expensive and very labour saving. Most can be given a home-made flavour by adding individual touches.

(1) Mushroom soup; add mushrooms, or even mushroom stalks if you have them, chopped and softened in butter over a low heat, with cream and a dusting of chopped chives.

(2) Tomato soup: skin and chop 2 tomatoes, soften in butter with a small chopped onion and half a teaspoon of sugar. Add at the last moment with a little cream. A crushed clove of garlic is a delicious addition.

(3) Packet Scotch Broth, or any brown soup can be boosted by adding left-over stew, home-made stock or cooked vegetables, or chop a small onion very fine, fry till golden brown and add.

(4) Packet Chicken or Spring Vegetable soups are improved if you use stock made from chicken bones simmered in water for 2 hours. If you have any chicken meat left, chop it finely

and add with parsley, or pour a little cream in just before serving.

(5) Tomato, mushroom and clear soups have more flavour if you add 1 tablespoon of sherry to each 900 ml (1½ pints) just before serving.

(6) Oxtail soup gets a lift from a squeeze of lemon, and a tablespoon of port added at the last moment, or some fried onion.

(7) Cream soups: cut some Cheddar or Gruyere cheese into small cubes and drop a few into each serving to give an unusual texture and flavour. An excellent supper dish for children.

Clear Soups

Clear Beef, Chicken and Spring Vegetable soups are best before a main course which includes something with a creamy consistency, for instance, haddock in cheese sauce, pork steaks with mushrooms in creamy gravy, or cauliflower with white sauce.

EASY CLEAR BEEF SOUP (serves 4-6)

2 Knorr Beef cubes
2 tablesp. sherry
1 carrot cut into short fine strips

1¼ l (2 pints) water
1 dessertsp. chopped parsley
1 small onion chopped fine
25 g (1 oz) butter

Soften carrot and onion in butter over a low heat, with the lid on the pan, for 15 minutes. Dissolve beef cubes in hot water, bring to the boil, add carrot and onion, sherry and parsley. Serve immediately. Never before beef or steak.

HOT CHEESE STRAWS ARE VERY GOOD WITH THIS:

90 g (3 oz) grated Cheddar cheese
1 egg yolk
1 dessertsp. water

45 g (1½ oz) butter
90 g (3 oz) flour
salt, pepper and ½ teasp. dry mustard

Sift the flour, cut the butter into little squares and rub into the flour until it is like bread crumbs. Add cheese, salt, pepper and mustard, and mix well by letting the dry mixture run through your fingers. Work in egg yolk and water until you have a smooth dough, roll out about $\frac{3}{4}$ cm ($\frac{1}{4}$ inch) thick on a floured board, cut into straws about $1\frac{1}{2}$ cm ($\frac{1}{2}$ inch) wide and bake in a medium oven till golden brown, about 10 minutes. Watch carefully as they brown suddenly. These can be made beforehand, and heated just before the meal.

CHICKEN NOODLE SOUP (serves 4-6)

$1\frac{1}{4}$ l (2 pints) home-made chicken stock, or 3 Knorr Chicken cubes and water.
1 tablesp. finely chopped parsley

2 tablesp. sherry (if liked).
1 dessertsp. noodles or pasta rings.

Bring stock, or water with cubes added, to the boil, add noodles or pasta rings, boil for 7 minutes until just tender to bite. Add parsley and sherry, serve at once as noodles are apt to get soggy. Never before any chicken dish.

Cream Soups

Cream soups are all basically the same, a vegetable steamed in butter and a little water, which is then sieved, or whizzed up in the electric blender, a great time saver. Milk and cream, and sometimes flour, add to the smooth rich texture. Never serve before a creamy second course; good before grilled or fried fish or meat. Bread cubes about $1\frac{1}{2}$ cm ($\frac{1}{2}$ inch) square fried till crisp and golden brown in oil or fat, are a pleasant accompaniment. Rashers fried till crisp, then crumbled on to the soup are even nicer.

CREAM OF CARROT SOUP (serves 4-6)

5 large carrots
900 ml ($1\frac{1}{2}$ pints) chicken stock (made with Knorr cubes will do)
300 ml ($\frac{1}{2}$ pint) milk
1 tablesp. finely chopped parsley

250 g ($\frac{1}{2}$ lb) tomatoes
150 ml ($\frac{1}{4}$ pint) cream
75 (3 oz) butter
Salt and pepper

Scrape and slice carrots, add to melted butter in stewpan, and cook very slowly for 10 minutes, shaking pan frequently to stop browning. To peel tomatoes pour boiling water on them, leave for 20 seconds, then put in cold water. Add peeled quartered tomatoes, with the pips squeezed out and discarded, to the carrots and cook gently for another 2 minutes. Now add hot chicken stock, salt and pepper, cover closely with tinfoil as well as the saucepan lid, and simmer till carrots are soft, about 40 minutes. Rub through a sieve, or liquidize in blender, bring to boiling point. Taste for seasoning, add milk and cream (or top milk), reheat but do not let it boil, sprinkle with chopped parsley and serve. This soup is a delicate tangerine colour which is very unusual.

CREAM OF MUSHROOM SOUP (serves 4-6)

250 g (½ lb) mushrooms (old black ones discolour the soup)
1 sprig parsley, thyme and a bay leaf
900 ml (1½ pints) chicken stock (or 1 Knorr chicken cube and water)
50 g (2 oz) butter
600 ml (1 pint) milk
50 g (2 oz) flour
Salt and paprika pepper
2 tablesp. cream or top milk
3 teasp. mushroom Ketchup (optional)

Wipe mushrooms with a damp cloth, avoid peeling them as much of the flavour is in the skin. Melt butter in a saucepan, add sliced mushrooms, including stalks, cover closely and cook over a very low heat for about 8 minutes. Blend flour to a smooth paste with a little of the chicken stock, add to mushrooms with the rest of the stock and the herbs. Simmer for another 7 or 8 minutes before adding the milk, reheat but do not boil, taste for seasoning, pour cream into individual soup cups, add hot soup and dust with paprika pepper, this makes a pleasant colour contrast. Mushroom Ketchup sharpens the flavour. Leave this soup unsieved with little bits of mushroom floating in it, or put it through the blender before the milk is added, if a smooth soup is wanted. Good with small cubes of potato, fried till crisp and golden.

Broth

Broth, which needs very long slow cooking, is really the liquid in which mutton, beef, chicken or bacon has been stewed with various vegetables. Often the meat is removed and served separately, but it is very good as a main course in winter if the meat is cut up small and put back.

Dumplings add bulk and flavour to all types of broth, and are made like this:

200 g (½ lb) flour   1 egg, a pinch salt
a little cold water

Knead the egg into the flour and salt, adding enough water to make a stiff dough. Form this into little balls the size of marbles, and drop into the boiling broth 15 minutes before dishing up. Cover closely, and do not lift the lid again until ready to serve. Chopped parsley or a pinch of herbs added to the dough give more flavour.

BEEF BROTH (serves 6)

1 kg (2 lb) shin of beef   1¾ l (3 pints) cold water
1 carrot and 1 onion   ½ a turnip, ¼ small cabbage
1 tablesp. pearl barley   50 g (2 oz) butter
salt and pepper

Cut beef into pieces, brown in butter, add water and seasoning, and simmer, closely covered, over a low heat for 2 hours. Skim off all fat and scum, then add barley and the chopped vegetables and continue to cook slowly for another hour. Taste for seasoning and serve steaming hot.

MUTTON BROTH (serves 6)

This is made exactly the same as Beef Broth, only substituting 1 kg (2 lb) neck of mutton, cut into neat pieces and trimmed of fat, for the shin of beef.

OXTAIL SOUP (serves 6)

1 oxtail	1 carrot
25 g (1 oz) fat	3 stalks of celery
2 onions	1¾ l (3 pints) stock or water
50 g (2 oz) streaky bacon	1 tablesp. raisins
3 cloves	1 bay leaf
chopped parsley	1 tablesp. port (optional)
1 clove garlic (optional)	25 g (1 oz) flour
Salt and pepper	1 tablesp. lemon juice

Ask the butcher to chop the oxtail into segments. Wash and
dry, cut off excess fat. Put into heavy saucepan with fat to
brown, then add chopped bacon, onions, carrot and celery,
and sweat for 10 minutes over low heat with the lid on. Pour
on stock, season with salt and pepper, add raisins, cloves and
the bay leaf and leave to simmer gently for 3½ hours until the
meat comes off the bones.

Skim off the fat and remove the bones, cloves and bay leaf.
Put back meat cut into small pieces, add flour mixed into a
smooth paste with a little stock, and boil for 10 minutes. Adjust
seasoning, flavour with garlic crushed to a paste, lemon juice
and port, and dust with chopped parsley. Very rich and
warming.

Fish Soup

SMOKED HADDOCK SOUP (serves 4-6)

500 g (1 lb) smoked haddock	2 medium onions
1 medium potato	50 g (2 oz) butter
Salt and pepper	600 ml. (1 pint) milk
1¾ l (2 pints) water	3 tablesp. cream or 'top milk'.

Fry chopped vegetables in half the butter for 5 minutes over
low heat, then simmer, closely covered, with the water until all
is soft. Skin the haddock and simmer with the vegetables until
it flakes up easily. Remove the fish bones, sieve the mixture
carefully or put through the blender, and return to the saucepan with the milk. Adjust the seasoning, (remember that the
haddock was salty to start with) bring to boiling point, stir in
cream and remaining butter, and serve.

A handful of shelled shrimps gives a luxury touch; or this

soup makes a delicious supper dish served with Cheesy Crisps made like this: fry rounds of bread until crisp and golden, put a teaspoon of grated cheese on each and brown in a hot oven or under the grill.

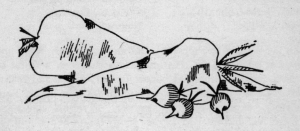

Fish

'Surrounded entirely by water' as we are in Ireland there is a great choice of fish at reasonable prices as well as the more expensive luxuries; and fish makes a good alternative to meat in the main course.

There are many kinds of fish: cod, hake halibut, whiting, sole and plaice are all white fish which is easy on the digestion and suits babies, old people and invalids. Children who are growing and need a great deal of energy benefit from oily fish such as herrings and mackerel which are nourishing and cheap. Salmon is also an oily fish caught both in salt and fresh water. Trout, perch and pike are all fresh water fish. Smoked haddock and kippers add variety and keep well. Shellfish have a delicious delicate flavour and unusual texture, but are expensive.

Be sure to choose your fish carefully. If it is freshly caught the skin will be shiny and moist, the eyes bulging and bright, the backbone stiff and the flesh firm to touch. Also there will be no fishy smell – the word 'fishy' has come literally to mean 'of dubious character', so take heed! Your fishmonger will usually gut the fish and fillet it too, if you ask him.

If you have to clean it yourself, wash it under the tap, scrape gently from tail to nose with a knife to remove the scales (if of scaled variety), then cut the head off. Slit the underside open from the vent upwards with a sharp pointed knife or kitchen scissors, and pull out the insides. Keep the roe if there is any, it lies in sacs on either side of the backbone. Scrape all the blood away from the backbone under cold running water, and rub the black skin away from the inside with salt, as both these give a bitter taste.

For each person buy: (a) about 220 g ($\frac{1}{2}$ lb) white fish like cod or hake; (b) two medium fillets of sole or plaice; (c) a whole mackerel or herring, or two if the fish are small or the appetites large.

Under-cooked fish tastes slimy; you will know the fish is ready if the flesh comes easily from the bone, and flakes apart, and if the backbone protrudes a little at each end.

Ways with Fish

(1)*Frying* Suitable for (a) cod, fresh haddock, hake and turbot which are cut into steaks about 3 cm (1 inch) thick. (b) Medium sized sole, plaice, trout, mackerel and herrings which are fried whole, or as fillets. Herrings and mackerel can have two slanting cuts on each side to speed up cooking.

Method: Dry the fish well, dip in milk and coat with either egg and fresh bread crumbs; flour; or oatmeal. Heat the fat, which should be at least 5 cm (2 inches) deep in a heavy pan, to the point where a crust of bread will form little bubbles and rise to the top when dropped in. Allow about 5 to 7 minutes each side, lift out carefully, test to see it is done, and drain on kitchen paper. Oil is also suitable for frying, but not butter as it burns easily – if the fat is not hot enough your fish will be greasy and broken, not crisp outside and flaky inside. Garnish with wedges of lemon and parsley. Appropriate vegetables: French beans, peas or tomatoes and small crisp chips.

(2) *Fish Baked in a Parcel* (a) whole trout and mackerel or steaks of white fish are seasoned and wrapped in individual parcels of oiled greaseproof paper or in silver foil, placed in a roasting tin and baked in a moderately hot oven 205° C (gas mark 6) for about 20 to 25 minutes. (b) Whole large fish such as cod, fresh haddock or salmon are baked in the same way with a little chopped onion, a bay leaf and a nut of butter included in the parcel. Allow 25 minutes for the first $\frac{1}{2}$ kg (1 lb) and 5 minutes for each extra $\frac{1}{2}$ kg (1 lb). Remove skin and serve

with Hollandaise, Tartare, Egg or Caper Sauce, or Mayonnaise.
Appropriate vegetables: Peas or grilled tomatoes and baked
potatoes in their jackets, which are done in the oven at the
same time.

(3) *Fish Cooked in Butter*   Good for small trout, sole, plaice
or salmon cutlets.

Method: Dry the fish, coat in seasoned flour and place in
frying pan with butter which is smoking hot, but not browned.
Lower the heat at once and allow fish to simmer slowly for
about 10 minutes on each side, more if thick. When done the
fish should be flaky inside, golden and buttery outside. Drain
and serve sprinkled with chopped parsley, and garnish with
lemon wedges. Serve with brown butter which is made the
following way: heat 50 g (2 oz.) butter in a small saucepan over
a very low heat until it is the colour of hazel nuts, watching
very carefully as butter 'catches' easily (in this case use it
anyway because it will have turned into Black Butter, which is
slightly darker than Brown Butter). Any slightly sour sauce is
good too – Tartare, Hollandaise or Rua. Suitable vegetables:
spinach, peas or matchstick carrots, and fluffy mashed potato.

(4) *Boiled or Poached Fish*   Suitable for whole salmon, codling,
fresh haddock or wrasse: or for portions of middle cut of these
fish.

Method: Wrap whole or part of fish in greaseproof paper
and place in a fish kettle or saucepan in hot water, to which salt
has been added at the rate of 50 g (2 oz) to each litre (quart).
A bay leaf, one dessertsp. of vinegar or white wine, and a little
sliced onion can be added to each litre (quart) for extra flavour
if wanted. Bring to the boil, cover, and simmer very gently
allowing 10 to 12 minutes to every 500 g (1 lb), lift out carefully, drain and remove skin. Serve on a hot dish with butter
dotted over. Nice with Shrimp or Caper Sauce, mushrooms
and tomatoes cooked in butter, and potatoes boiled in their
skins.

(5) *Grilled Fish*   Small fish like trout, mackerel and herring
are good grilled.

Method: Wash and dry the cleaned fish, which can be left whole, or split along the backbone so it lies flat. Brush over with melted butter or oil, season and place on the rack in the grill pan (if you have a sheet of foil underneath it saves washing up!) preheat the grill and grill at moderate heat, allowing 5 to 8 minutes for each side, or if the fish is split grill only one side, skin side down. Serve with lemon, raw tomatoes and left over boiled potatoes, sliced and fried in butter.

(6) *Baked Fish* Suitable for a whole, or a portion of, cod, hake or fresh haddock which can be stuffed; fish cutlets or fillets of plaice.

Method: Butter a roasting tin or casserole, arrange prepared fish in it and pour over half and half water and milk, or water and white wine to a depth of 1½ cm (½ inch). Dot the fish with butter, season and add a bay leaf and cover with silver foil folded over the edges of the tin, or the lid on the casserole. Bake in a moderately hot oven (205° C gas mark 6) for 30 minutes for the first 500 g (1 lb) and 5 minutes for each extra 500 g (1 lb). Remove skin and serve coated with Mushroom, Cheese or Shrimp Sauce. Suitable vegetables are baby marrow cooked with onion, and potatoes in their jackets which are baked at the same time as the fish.

INEXPENSIVE FISH CAKES (serves 6)

500 g (1 lb) cooked white fish
500 g (1 lb) cooked mashed
  potato
1 dessertsp. chopped parsley
salt and pepper

2 beaten eggs
1 dessertsp. finely chopped
  onion

For coating: a little flour, one egg and fresh white breadcrumbs. For frying: oil or fat.

Flake fish and remove skin and bones, mix with potato, onion, parsley, seasoning and beaten egg. Divide into 6 portions, shaping each into a round flat cake. Roll in the flour, dip into beaten egg, coat all over with breadcrumbs using a palette knife to pat them firmly in place. Fry until crisp, about

8 minutes each side. Good with bottled tomato sauce, cauliflower in white sauce and chips.

INEXPENSIVE FISH LOAF (serves 6)

500 g (1 lb) cooked white fish
2 tablesp. fresh white breadcrumbs
1 tablesp. finely chopped onion
1 teasp. Anchovy Essence (optional)

500 g (1 lb) cooked mashed potato
2 beaten eggs
salt and pepper

Mix all ingredients together, shape into a loaf and place on a greased roasting tin. Criss-cross with a fork to make a pattern and bake in a moderately hot oven (205° C gas mark 6) for 40 minutes. Serve with mushroom or home-made tomato sauce (Sauce Rua, see below), good with buttered carrots and peas mixed together.

COD IN A PARCEL WITH SAUCE RUA (serves 4)

1 kg (2 lb) cod, hake or fresh haddock
25 g (1 oz) butter
1 bay leaf

Silver foil for wrapping fish
Lemon juice
Salt and pepper
Parsley and lemon wedges

Cod needs a little special attention before cooking, as otherwise it tends to resemble wet cottonwool. The texture is much improved if you wash and dry the portion of cod, rub in a little lemon juice and sprinkle with salt. Leave in a cool place for about 45 minutes to allow some of the liquid to drain off. Dry the fish once more, and proceed with recipe. Dot inside and out with butter, dust with salt and pepper and wrap, with a bay leaf, in foil or greaseproof paper, turning the ends under so the parcel is sealed. Bake in a moderate oven (195° C gas mark 5) for 30 to 35 minutes, unwrap, test to see the flesh flakes easily from the bone, and remove skin. Serve on a hot dish garnished with parsley and lemon.

SAUCE RUA

1 medium onion
¼ teasp. of sugar
salt and pepper
2 tablesp. tomato sauce

3 medium tomatoes
30 g (1 oz) butter
1 clove of garlic (optional)

Fry the chopped onion gently in butter, when just turning colour add tomatoes skinned and sliced, sugar, tomato sauce and salt and pepper. Crush a clove of garlic with a knife blade against a plate (or better still invest in a garlic press if you use it often). Add garlic, cover and simmer for 15 minutes. I like this sauce served 'chunky', or it may be put through the blender and served smooth and creamy.

COD, BAKED WITH BACON (serves 4-6)

1 kg (2 lb) cod	6 rashers of bacon
25 g (1 oz) butter	Lemon juice
Salt and pepper	150 ml (¼ pint) milk and
100 g (¼ lb) mushrooms	water mixed
Pinch of grated nutmeg	Chopped chives

Cut the cod into steaks about 4 cm (1½ inches) thick, then rub with lemon juice and salt; leave for 45 minutes until surplus liquid has drained off. Dry the steaks, season with salt and pepper and a sprinkle of nutmeg and place in a buttered fireproof dish with chopped mushroom stalks. Dot with butter, pour over milk and water mixed, and lay rashers neatly over all. Bake in a moderately hot oven (205° C gas mark 6) for about 30 minutes, covering with foil if the bacon is getting over-done. Serve in the dish in which it was cooked, garnish with mushrooms fried in butter, and chopped chives. Goes well with tomatoes, halved and baked in the oven for 10 minutes, and rice boiled with a few sultanas and a pinch of turmeric which gives a lovely yellow colour.

Cod is also good fried, cooked in butter, or baked.

SMOKED HADDOCK WITH SAUCE (serves 4-6)

1 kg (2 lb) smoked haddock	50 g (2 oz) butter
50 g (2 oz) flour	500 ml (1 pint) milk
salt and pepper	2 tomatoes
50 g (2 oz) grated Cheddar cheese	

Put the fish in a saucepan with enough cold water to cover, bring to the boil and simmer until it is tender. Drain well and flake the fish, removing all skin and bones. While the haddock is cooking make the sauce: melt the butter over a low heat, add flour and mix into a smooth paste with a wooden spoon, gradually adding the milk. Continue stirring, and boil for about 5 minutes until the sauce is smooth and of a coating consistency. Season with salt and pepper, pour over flaked haddock and put the mixture into a buttered ovenproof dish about 8 cm (3 inches) deep. Skin and slice the tomatoes arranging them in a pattern on the top of the mixture, scatter grated cheese over and bake in a moderately hot oven (205° C gas mark 6) until the cheese is brown and melted, or brown under the grill.

HADDOCK KEDGEREE (serves 4-6)

500 g (1 lb) cooked smoked haddock
75 g (3 oz) butter
220 g (8 oz) patna rice
2 tablesp. chopped parsley

1 medium onion
1 tablesp. curry powder (optional)
2 hard boiled eggs

Fry the finely chopped onion in half the butter until golden, in a saucepan. Add the rice and pour in 45 ml (¾ pint) of boiling water. Boil rice until tender (about 12 to 14 minutes); if water is all absorbed before this, add a little more. Melt the remaining butter, add in the flaked fish sprinkled with curry powder, and the rice, stirring very gently with a fork to keep the mixture crumbly. Chop the egg whites and add; spoon all into a hot serving dish. Sieve the hard boiled egg yolks over the fish mixture and scatter chopped parsley over all. Tinned or fresh salmon are also excellent in kedgeree. A good breakfast dish.

HERRINGS BAKED WITH VEGETABLES
(serves 6, inexpensive)

6 large herrings filleted
200 g (½ lb) boiled potatoes
25 g (1 oz) butter
Salt and pepper

1 medium onion
1 bay leaf
6 tomatoes
Chopped parsley

Butter a fireproof dish, slice the potatoes and put them in a layer on the bottom. Season the fillets with salt and pepper and lay on the potato, chop the onion and sprinkle evenly over, then season again and add a layer of skinned sliced tomato. Add the bay leaf and chopped parsley, dot with butter and bake for about 35 minutes in a moderately hot oven (205° C gas mark 6) until the fish is flaky.

A good supper dish, follow with Rhubarb or Apple Crumble and custard, baked at the same time.

Herrings are good coated in oatmeal and fried; or grilled.

KIPPERS WITH BUTTER

1 or 2 plump kippers for each person
1 teasp. of butter for each kipper

Place the kippers head to tail in a roasting pan, pour boiling water over to cover, and cook in a moderate oven (195° C gas mark 5) for 5 to 7 minutes. Remove from water and drain, serve with a nut of butter on each kipper. Much more succulent than fried kippers. They can be done in the same way over medium heat in a frying pan closely covered.

MACKEREL, GRILLED WITH MUSTARD

1 or 2 mackerel for each person   Salt and pepper
Made mustard   Tomato sauce

Be careful to choose fresh mackerel as they 'go off' very quickly. Dry the prepared fish, cut off the heads and tails, then make three slanting incisions on each side. Spread about half a teaspoon of made mustard into each incision, salt and pepper the fish, lay on the rack in a grill pan lined with foil to save washing up, and grill for about 8 minutes each side, until the flesh lifts off the backbone. If cooking for large numbers of hungry people I usually, prepare the fish with mustard and bake in a roasting pan for 15 minutes instead of grilling, as it's quicker. (205° C gas mark 6). Mackerel can also be boiled, fried or baked in a parcel.

BAKED PERCH WITH FRESH TOMATO SAUCE
(serves 4-6)

Although perch are plentiful in the lakes and rivers of Ireland you are unlikely to come by them unless there is a fisherman in the family, so first catch your perch!

| 1 medium to large perch | 25 g (1 oz) butter |
| salt and pepper | |

For Fresh Tomato Sauce (my own recipe)

3 medium peeled tomatoes	½ teasp. sugar
1 teasp. chopped raw onion	2 tablesp. cream cheese
a good pinch of salt	a pinch of Cayenne pepper

Clean the fish and cut off the head and tail; no need to scale it. Dry, dot with butter, dust with salt and pepper and wrap in tinfoil. Bake in a roasting pan in a moderate oven (195° C gas mark 5) for 25 to 40 minutes according to weight. Unwrap, remove skin and serve on an oval dish. The flesh is very firm and white. To make fresh tomato sauce: Liquidize the tomatoes with chopped onion, salt, pepper, sugar and cream cheese. A crushed clove of garlic (if liked) adds piquancy. Serve separately in a sauceboat.

PLAICE OR SOLE WITH BUTTER AND GREEN
GRAPES (serves 4-6)

8 medium fillets of plaice or sole	90 g (3 oz) butter
1 dessertsp. lemon juice	100 g (¼ lb) green grapes
Salt and pepper	a little flour
1 tablesp. chopped parsley	

Peel and pip the grapes, sprinkle with lemon juice. Wash and dry the plaice, roll in seasoned flour and fry gently in half the butter until golden brown. Lift out carefully and place in a serving dish. Clean the pan, put in the remaining butter and heat till foaming, add the chopped parsley (reserving a little for the garnishing), the lemon juice and seasoning, and pour it at once over the fish. Garnish with the grapes and the remaining parsley. A very delicately flavoured dish, it goes well with mushrooms and grilled tomato, and mashed potato sprinkled with paprika to give colour contrast.

Plaice and sole are delicious coated with egg and fresh breadcrumbs and fried; baked in a casserole, or grilled.

SALMON

Salmon is the king of fish, very expensive early in the season,
but in Ireland the price often drops sharply in June when the
young salmon, called grilse or peal, are plentiful. The flesh is a
delicate pink and very filling, so that 170 g (6 oz) for each
person is enough; though people will eat more if there is more.
It is lovely to be lavish with it at a party! The head and tail and
insides are nearly one quarter of the total weight, so allow for
this when buying a whole fish.

SALMON BAKED IN A PARCEL, WITH
HOLLANDAISE SAUCE (serves 4-6)

1 kg (2 lb) middle cut of salmon	or a small grilse
½ a small onion	1 small carrot
1 bay leaf	Salt and pepper
oil or melted butter for brushing	1 lemon

Clean carefully, but there is no need to scale the fish, just brush
it with oil or melted butter, and wrap it up in silverfoil or
greaseproof paper with the sliced onion, carrot, bay leaf and
a good sprinkling of salt and pepper. Bake in a moderately hot
oven (205° C gas mark 6) for 30 to 40 minutes, test to see that
the flesh lifts easily from the backbone, remove the skin carefully, leaving the delicious brown flesh beneath the skin which
is full of flavour and gives a rich colour contrast. Serve whole
on a hot dish, garnish with lemon slices, sliced stuffed olives
and parsley. Hollandaise Sauce, page 103.

Salmon cooked like this deserves the best of company: fresh
young garden peas with mint, and delicious small new potatoes
tossed in butter; though frozen peas carefully cooked, and
fluffy mashed potato will do. As salmon is filling, follow with
a very light sweet.

Salmon steaks are delicious cooked slowly in butter, or
grilled, and cuts of salmon can also be boiled or baked.

SALMON MAYONNAISE

Cooked salmon, lemon wedges and parsley; lettuce, hard boiled
eggs, sliced cucumber, tomatoes, radishes or whatever salad
vegetables are in season. Ingredients for Mayonnaise are:

3 egg yolks	300 ml (½ pint) olive oil
3 teasp. lemon juice or wine	1 teasp. salt
vinegar	½ teasp. pepper

Have all the ingredients at room temperature, and rinse the
mixing bowl in hot water, drying well before use. Put the
yolks of eggs in the bowl with the salt and pepper and one
teaspoon of lemon juice or wine vinegar, mix well together. I
find the electric hand mixer, running at it's lowest speed, very
useful for making Mayonnaise, but many people prefer a
wooden spoon. Add the oil very slowly, drop by drop at first,
mixing all the time so that the oil is completely absorbed and
the mixture gets very thick. Once this consistency is reached,
mix in another teaspoon of lemon juice or wine vinegar, and
then the oil may be added more rapidly in a thin stream, or a
tablespoon at a time, still beating continuously. When all the
oil has been added, beat in the remaining teaspoon of lemon
juice or wine vinegar. Should the Mayonnaise curdle, it can be
rescued by starting from the beginning in a new basin with a
fresh egg yolk, and adding the curdled Mayonnaise by degrees.

Arrange the cooked salmon, broken into large flakes, on a
bed of crisp lettuce, garnish with sliced cucumber, lemon
wedges and parsley, and arrange the other salad vegetables
around. Serve Mayonnaise separately in a sauceboat.

SCALLOPED FISH

For individual servings, flake small quantities of any cooked
fish into scallop shells or small ovenproof dishes and spoon
over a little white sauce (page 103) flavoured with finely
chopped parsley and capers; or anchovy essence; or grated
cheese and a pinch of paprica. Sprinkle with grated cheese or
bread crumbs and brown under the grill or in the oven.

TROUT COOKED IN BUTTER (serves 4)

4 small trout	100 g (4 oz) butter
1 quartered lemon	Salt and pepper
Chopped parsley	A little flour

Dry the cleaned trout and roll them in seasoned flour. Heat three quarters of the butter in a large frying pan until hot but not brown, put in trout and remove pan to low heat. Cook the trout very gently for about 6 minutes each side, until the flesh lifts easily from the bone, place on a warm dish, sprinkle with parsley and garnish with quartered lemon. Add the remaining butter to the pan, heat till foaming and pour over the fish. Good with grilled tomatoes and lightly mashed potatoes. Mushrooms on very crisp fried bread make a nice contrast as a second course. Trout may also be fried, baked in a parcel or grilled.

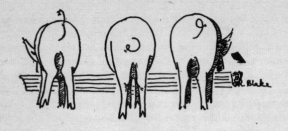

Meat

When buying meat ask your butcher's advice, but also learn to use your own judgment. Choose the type and quality of meat most suitable to the way in which you are going to cook it; on the whole the most expensive cuts of meat are the most straightforward and easy to prepare. However there are many economical cuts which are delicious and tender if cooked with care and imagination. One word of warning: some cheaper cuts may contain such a high proportion of fat or bone to meat, that they actually work out more expensive per portion, especially if you take the length of preparation and cooking time into account.

Ways with Meat

(1) *Braising* suitable for any joint which needs long slow cooking such as topside or rump of beef, and best end of neck or leg of mutton. The meat is cooked by a combination of slow heat, and the steam, which is retained by close covering. Use a heavy pan with a tightly fitting lid, or there are some colourfully enamelled cast-iron casseroles on the market which are especially designed to come straight from the cooker to the table.

Method: heat two tablespoons of cooking oil in a heavy saucepan or cast-iron casserole, put in the joint weighing about 1½ to 2 kg (3 to 4½ lb) and brown it on both sides, remove and keep hot. Slice 1 carrot, $\frac{1}{2}$ a swede turnip, 2 large onions and 2 or 3 sticks of celery and brown them in the oil for 6 to 8 minutes, replace the meat and add about 450 ml ($\frac{3}{4}$ pint) stock or water. Cover closely with greaseproof paper or foil as well as the lid, and simmer very gently over low heat, or preferably in a slow oven (170° C gas mark 3) until the meat is tender (about $2\frac{1}{2}$-$3\frac{1}{2}$ hours) – insert a metal skewer and if it comes out easily the meat is ready. Baste occasionally with the stock, and add a little more liquid if needed.

Various herbs such as bayleaf, parsley or crushed garlic add flavour, and a few rashers of cheap flank bacon cut into strips will help to tenderize almost fatless meat such as topside of beef.

Serve the meat on a hot dish with the vegetables, strain and skim the stock (mutton particularly is apt to be fatty), thicken with a little flour if liked, and pour over the meat. Accompany with boiled potatoes and a green vegetable. Meat cooked this way is delicious as none of the good meat juices are lost, they are all there flavouring the gravy; this also applies to stews.

(2) *Stewing*   suitable for the cheaper, coarser cuts of meat such as round steak, shin, neck and topside of beef; scrag end, shoulder, loin and breast of veal; shoulder and neck of mutton.

Method: Very similar to braising but cut the meat into 3 cm (1 inch) cubes. Use a heavy saucepan with a well fitting lid, or a cast-iron or ovenproof glass casserole. If making a brown stew, brown the pieces of beef or mutton in a little oil or fat before adding the stock, a white stew is made of veal or lamb and the meat is usually soaked in cold water for a few hours before cooking.

Add only a little liquid: 450 ml ($\frac{3}{4}$ pint) is enough for about 1 kg (2 lb) of meat, season and cover with greaseproof paper or foil as well as the lid. Simmer very slowly over low heat, or in a slow oven (170° C gas mark 3) for about $1\frac{1}{2}$ hours then add the prepared vegetables and simmer for another hour. Herbs such as garlic, rosemary and oregano bring out the flavour of mutton, red wine in place of a little of the stock is good with beef. Stews must be carefully skimmed, especially if fatty, and a little flour may be added to thicken the stock.

(3) *Roasting* suitable for sirloin, ribs, wing ribs and top rump of beef; shoulder, loin, leg and best end of neck of lamb, mutton and veal; and loin, spare rib, leg and belly of pork.

Method: (a) the classic way of roasting is to rub the joint with salt and pepper, place in a meat dish on a wire rack, and add two tablespoons of fat or dripping. Put into a pre-heated, very hot oven (230° C gas mark 8) for 15 to 20 minutes until the outside is brown and crisp – the aim is to sear it and thus prevent the loss of moisture with resulting shrinking of the joint. Then lower the heat to moderate (195° C gas mark 5) and baste frequently for the remainder of the cooking time.

Cooking times

Beef: allow 15 to 20 minutes per ½ kg (1 lb), add 20 minutes at the end.

Mutton: 20 minutes per ½ kg (1 lb), add 20 minutes at the end.

Lamb: same as mutton.

Veal: allow 25 minutes per ½ kg (1lb), add 25 minutes at the end.

Pork: allow 30 minutes per ½ kg (1 lb), add 30 minutes at the end.

Chicken and duck: allow 20 minutes to the ½ kg (1 lb).

Test with a skewer: for beef if the juice runs red it is underdone, if faintly pink it is ready; for mutton, lamb, veal, pork and poultry the juice should be colourless when the meat is done. Remove the meat onto a hot dish, and keep hot.

To make the gravy: carefully pour off the fat from the meat dish retaining the dark meat juices, sprinkle in about one dessertspoon of flour, scrape up the sediment and mix in about 300 ml (½ pint) of vegetable water or stock, boil for about 3 minutes and strain into a gravyboat. This method of roasting gives a delicious flavour, particularly to the outside slices of meat, but there is considerable shrinkage and loss of weight which may be up to a quarter of the whole, and a small joint may become very dry and tough. Many people now prefer to roast their meat wrapped in a parcel as there is little wastage and the meat is more succulent and tender.

Method: (b) to roast meat in a parcel, brush the meat with oil or melted butter, and wrap in two thicknesses of greaseproof paper or one of foil, turning the ends under to seal the

parcel. Bake in a pre-heated moderate oven (195° C gas mark 5)
until 30 minutes before the end of cooking time, remove the
paper and baste the joint. Sprinkle a little flour and salt over
the joint and leave to brown for remaining cooking time, serve
on a hot dish.

Cooking time: due to the wrapping this is longer, allow 30
minutes more than the normal total roasting time for beef and
veal, and 40 minutes more for mutton, lamb and pork.

(4) *Boiling* Suitable for salt meats such as ham, bacon, ox
tongue, corned beef and pickled pork; and for fresh meat such
as leg of mutton, boiling beef or rather elderly fowl.

Method: (a) for salt meat. If very salty, soak in cold water
for a few hours, then put into fresh cold water and bring
slowly to the boil, simmer very gently.

Method: (b) for fresh meat. Put into boiling salted water
and boil rapidly for 5 minutes to harden the outside layer of
meat – this will prevent the good juices escaping into the water
which will be thrown away. Then lower the heat and simmer
very gently so that the water is barely bubbling. If it boils too
hard after the first 5 minutes the meat will turn out tough and
fibrous all through.

Cooking time for salt and fresh meat:
Allow 25 minutes to $\frac{1}{2}$ kg (1 lb) and add 25 minutes at the end,
test with a metal skewer, if it comes out easily the meat is ready.

About $1\frac{1}{4}$ hours before the end of cooking time add the
vegetables such as sliced carrot, swede turnip, parsnip, onion
and celery; herbs for flavouring and salt if needed.

(5) *Grilling* Suitable for tender cuts like rump, fillet or
undercut of beef; lamb and mutton chops from the loin,
chump and best end of neck; veal chops, cutlets and fillet;
and pork chops from the loin and chump and pieces of fillet,
also portions of chicken, sausages, kidneys and liver. Be sure
to cook the vegetables for the meal before the meat as this
should be eaten straight from the grill.

Method: preheat the grill and grill pan. Brush the meat with
oil, but do not salt it or it will make the juices run. Place on the
rack under the grill, about 9 cm (3 inches) away from the

source of heat, and brown rapidly on both sides to seal in the juices. Then lower the heat and grill until done, turning over if necessary and being careful not to prick the meat. Sprinkle with salt, and garnish with savoury butter, flavoured with parsley and lemon juice, or crushed garlic.

Grilling times
Steak 3 cm (1 inch) thick 6 to 8 minutes for rare, 10 to 12 minutes for medium
Cutlets and chops 3 cm (1 inch) thick 7 to 10 minutes
Pork chops 3 cm (1 inch) thick 12 to 16 minutes
Lambs kidneys 6 to 8 minutes
Sausages 7 to 8 minutes
Portion of chicken 10 to 15 minutes each side

A good alternative to grilling, particularly for steak, is to dry fry the meat in a heavy frying pan. Heat the pan, add about two teaspoons of oil to prevent the meat sticking, then put in the meat patting it down with a palette knife. Brown for about two minutes on one side, turn without pricking the meat, brown on the other side, then lower the heat a little and cook until tender. This method is about two minutes quicker than grilling as the heat is more direct. Sprinkle with salt and garnish with savoury butter.

(6) *Frying* Suitable for chops, liver, kidneys, sausages and portions of chicken.
Method: use fat, oil, or a mixture of oil and butter; margarine is not satisfactory as it tends to harden the meat. Always heat the fat or oil before adding the meat, or it will absorb the fat and become soggy and undigestable. The meat may be dipped in flour, or egg and breadcrumbs, or left uncoated. Put into the pan to brown on both sides over fairly quick heat, then lower the heat and cook until tender, season and drain on kitchen paper.

Beef

Beef should be dark red in colour, with a mottling of pale yellow fat through the flesh. Meat from very lean animals is apt to be dry and tough for it is the fat which keeps meat juicy and tender as it cooks. The presence of gristle suggests that the animal was aged. Beef must be well hung before use, check this with the butcher.

ROAST RIBS OR SIRLOIN OF BEEF
(serves 6 to 7)

2 kg. (4 to 4½ lb) sirloin or rib of beef; boned and rolled

2 tablesp. dripping   a little cooking oil

For Gravy: 1 dessertsp. port (optional)

1 tablesp. flour   Salt and pepper

450 ml (¾ pint) water or stock

Accompaniments, Yorkshire puffs, roast potatoes, green vegetable and horseradish sauce.

Salt and pepper the meat, and brush over with oil. Wrap in two thicknesses of greaseproof paper or one of foil, turn ends under and place on a rack in the meat tin, with two tablespoons of dripping. Bake in a preheated moderate oven (195° C gas mark 5) for about 2¼ hours or about 20 minutes less if liked rare, there is no need to baste. Test with a skewer, the juice should be faintly pink for medium done. 30 minutes before the end of cooking time, remove the wrapping, sprinkle with a little flour, salt and pepper, and brown for remaining cooking time low in the oven leaving room for the Yorkshire Puffs to be cooked on the top shelf of the oven.

The potatoes should be peeled and dried, then put into the meat tin round the joint 1¾ hours before the end of cooking time and sprinkled with salt. Baste two or three times, turn once to ensure even cooking.

For the gravy: remove the joint and keep hot, pour off most of the fat, brown the flour over medium heat stirring to mix in the delicious brown sediment, pour in 450 ml (¾ pint) stock or water in which vegetables have been cooked. Boil for about 3 minutes, stirring to get rid of the lumps, strain into a gravy dish and add port.

For Yorkshire Puffs:

100 g (4 oz) flour	1 egg
250 ml (½ pint) milk and water mixed	½ teasp. salt

Sift the flour and salt into a bowl, add the egg and a little liquid and mix, adding a little more milk and water at a time until the batter is thin and smooth. If using a hand mixer, put all the ingredients together in a bowl, and beat for about 5 minutes. Leave the batter to stand for about 30 minutes in a cool place.

Heat 12 patty tins, (the puffs will rise better in the straight sided kind), put one teaspoon of hot dripping from the meat tin and one tablespoon of batter into each, place in the top of the oven (220°C gas mark 7) and bake without opening the door for 20 to 25 minutes, when they should be crisp and golden.

Horseradish Sauce: the ready made horseradish sauce may be mixed half and half with whipped cream, adding a little mustard, and a squeeze of lemon juice.

The Real Thing: grate 2 tablesp. horseradish, mix with ½ teasp. mustard, salt, pepper, ½ teasp. sugar and 1 dessertsp. vinegar, stir carefully into 4 tablesp. whipped cream.

HUNGARIAN BEEF STEW OR GOULASH
(serves 4 to 6)

1 kg (2 lb) round steak	2 tablesp. dripping or oil
4 large onions	1 tablesp. flour
1 level dessertsp. paprika pepper	3 tomatoes
1 dessertsp. tomato purée	Salt and pepper
1 clove of garlic (optional)	Parsley and chives
600 ml (1 pint) stock	3 tablesp. yogurt

Accompaniments: boiled macaroni or pasta shells, or potatoes baked in their jackets at the same time as the stew. Heat the fat in a saucepan, brown the meat cut into 3 cm (1 inch) cubes, remove and keep hot. Fry the sliced onions until golden, add one dessertspoon paprika pepper (or more to taste), tomato puree, crushed garlic and the flour, stir and then pour in the stock. Bring to the boil, put back the meat, cover closely and simmer very gently over slow heat, or in a very moderate oven (180° C gas mark 4) for about 2 hours. Peel and slice the

tomatoes and add to the stew about two minutes before
dishing up. Finally, pour the yogurt over and serve with
boiled macaroni or floury potatoes.

BEEF AND MUSHROOM STEW WITH BREAD
TOPPING (serves 4)

750 g (1½ lb) stewing beef	2 tablesp. dripping
600 ml (1 pint) stock or water	1 tablesp. flour
1 clove garlic (optional)	1 large onion
100 g (¼ lb) mushrooms	½ teasp. sugar
1 sprig each parsley and thyme	Salt and pepper
1 tablesp. butter	1 pinch mace
3 thin slices of bread or	½ a Vienna loaf

Heat the fat in a saucepan, brown the meat cut into cubes, and
the chopped onion for about 8 minutes, turning frequently. Cut
the slices of bread into quarters, or slice the Vienna loaf,
leaving the crusts on in either case. Pour excess fat (if any)
from frying meat and onion over the bread, leave. Sprinkle
meat and onion mixture with flour, add hot stock, sugar, mace,
herbs, and salt and pepper to taste, then transfer to a casserole,
cover closely and stew in a very moderate oven (180° C gas
mark 4) for about 2 hours.

Remove the sprigs of parsley and thyme; skim off any fat,
and pour this also over the bread. Add mushrooms, previously
sliced through caps and stalks and fried in butter, to the stew,
arrange the bread over the top of the casserole pushing it down
into the gravy to get well soaked, it will rise to the top again.
Return stew to the oven, without the lid and bake for another
20 minutes until the bread is nice and brown. Children love
this stew.

STEAK AND KIDNEY PIE (serves 4 to 6)

1 kg (2 lb) stewing steak	1 ox kidney
450 ml (¾ pint) stock or water	1 large onion
1 tablesp. oil or dripping	2 cloves
a few mushrooms (optional)	Salt and pepper
220 g (½ lb) Rough Puff pastry	1 egg
(page 21)	

Heat the oil or dripping in a saucepan, fry the chopped onion until golden. Cut the meat into 3 cm (1 inch) cubes, and the kidney into small pieces, removing the white core. Add to the saucepan with the flour, cloves, stock and salt and pepper (fresh ground black pepper is best) and cover closely. Simmer gently over low heat or in a very moderate oven (180° C gas mark 4) for about 2 hours, add mushrooms fried in a little butter, pour into a pie dish and allow to cool.

Roll the pastry until it is a little larger than required, cut a narrow strip and lay it along the previously moistened edge of the pie dish, pressing down firmly. Brush with beaten egg, place the pastry top in position, press down along the edge and trim. Make a small hole in the centre to allow steam to escape, decorate with a few pastry leaves and brush with beaten egg mixed with a pinch of salt. Place the pie dish in a meat tin containing a little water (the steam from this will stop the pastry shrinking and falling into the dish) and bake in a moderately hot oven (205° C gas mark 6) for about half an hour, lower the heat to very moderate (180° C gas mark 4) and bake for 20 to 30 minutes more, covering if getting too brown. Delicious with fluffy mashed potato, brussels sprouts or savoury vegetable marrow.

Inexpensive Beef Dishes

SAVOURY OX KIDNEY (serves 4)

1 ox kidney	1 medium onion
6 rashers streaky bacon or flank	1 tablesp. sultanas
½ pkt. tomato soup mix	1 clove garlic (optional)
1 dessertsp. chopped parsley	25 g (1 oz) butter

Cut the ox kidney into small pieces, removing the white core. If the strong taste is disliked, put into a small bowl and pour boiling water over, leave for a few minutes, otherwise wash in cold water. Melt the butter in a saucepan, brown the bacon cut into strips with the chopped onion and kidney. Mix the half packet of tomato soup with 300 ml (½ pint) water pour this over the kidney mixture and add sultanas and the crushed clove of garlic, stir. Cover closely with greaseproof paper as well as the lid and simmer gently over low heat for about 30 minutes. Serve with boiled rice, or lightly mashed potatoes.

CURRIED MINCE (serves 4)

½ kg (1 lb) lean minced beef	1 slice white bread
25 g (1 oz) butter	1 large onion
1 tablesp. curry powder	½ teasp. sugar
1 teasp. salt	1 dessertsp. sultanas
8 almonds, chopped	1 egg
juice of half a lemon	1 cup of milk

Fry the chopped onion in the butter, add the curry powder, sugar, salt, lemon juice, sultanas and chopped almonds. Soak the bread in a little of the milk, mash with a fork and mix as lightly as possible with the minced beef and the curry mixture. Turn into a buttered pie dish and bake in a moderately slow oven (170° C gas mark 3) for 30 minutes. Beat the egg into ¾ of a cup of milk, add a pinch of salt and a little pepper, and pour over, return to the oven and bake for about 20 minutes more until the top is set. Serve with yellow rice and a glass of milk for each person. This is a traditional South African recipe, called Bobotie, and is very creamy in texture. Minced cooked beef or mutton may be used in place of the raw minced beef, and need only 35 minutes cooking in all.

STEWED OXTAIL (serves 3 to 4)

1 oxtail	2 tablesp. fat or butter
50 g (2 oz) flour	2 cloves
600 ml (1 pint) stock or water	1 onion
1 tablesp. lemon juice	4 large carrots
1 tablesp. raisins	Salt and pepper

Ask the butcher to cut the oxtail into pieces about 4 cm (1½ inches) long. Cut off as much fat as possible, wash the pieces of oxtail and dry them thoroughly. Melt the fat or butter in a saucepan, brown the pieces of oxtail, remove and keep hot. Fry the sliced onion until golden, add the flour, cloves, raisins, salt and pepper and stock or water, bring to the boil. Replace the pieces of oxtail, cover closely and simmer gently for 2 hours. Add the carrots cut into long slices, simmer again for another hour; skim off all the fat. Taste for seasoning, add the lemon juice, and serve with lots of mashed potato to mop up the delicious gravy. Small cubes of fried bread make a nice contrast for a garnish, too.

BOILED OXTONGUE (serves 6 to 7)

1 salted oxtongue	1 bayleaf
1 sprig each of parsley, rosemary, and sage	

Choose a tongue with a smooth skin as this will be young and tender, soak it for 3 to 4 hours in cold water, cut off excess fat. Place in a saucepan with cold water and the herbs and bring very slowly to the boil, simmer very gently for 2½ to 3½ hours, until tender. Leave to cool in the liquid, then remove the skin, and the little bones at the root of the tongue. Press the tongue into a medium sized pudding bowl, place a small saucer on top and then a heavy weight and leave overnight. Very delicious and tender; serve thinly sliced with salads, pickles and mayonnaise, combines well with cold chicken or ham.

Tongue may also be eaten hot, in which case, allow it to cool slightly in the water, remove skin and bones, and serve with tomato sauce, cauliflower or brussels sprouts, and mashed potato. It goes much further when pressed and served cold.

STEWED SHIN OF BEEF (serves 4)

½ kg (1 lb) shin of beef	2 tablesp. vinegar
1 large onion	2 carrots
Chopped parsley and chives	1 white turnip
450 ml (¾ pint) water	Salt and pepper
1 bayleaf	

Cut the meat into about 8 pieces, put them in a dish and pour the vinegar over with the chopped parsley and chives. Leave soaking at least an hour, turning several times. Then place them in a saucepan with the vinegar and herbs, add the water, bayleaf and salt and pepper, cover closely and simmer very gently over very low heat, or in a moderately slow oven (170° C gas mark 3) for 2 hours. Add the vegetables cut into thick slices and stew again for another hour. Serve with boiled potatoes, the gravy is rich and nourishing.

Veal

Veal should be pinkish in colour and has very little fat, so that it needs constant basting when cooking to keep it from becoming dry. It should be eaten fresh.

WHITE VEAL STEW (serves 4 to 6)

1 kg (2 lb) shoulder or breast of veal	2 large carrots
	1 onion
600 ml (1 pint) water or stock	2 leeks
1 sprig parsley and thyme	1 bayleaf
25 g (1 oz) butter	4 stalks celery
100 g (¼ lb) mushrooms	2 tablesp. flour
150 ml (¼ pint) cream	Pinch of mace
Juice of half a lemon	

Cut the meat into small pieces, leave to soak overnight with a little of the lemon juice. Put the veal into a saucepan with the stock or water, add salt and fresh ground black pepper and heat until it is boiling. Add the onion cut into four, the sliced carrots and leeks, celery and herbs, cover closely and simmer very gently over low heat, or in a moderately slow oven (170° C gas mark 3) for about 1½ hours, skim off any scum.

Mix the butter and the flour to a paste, stir this into the stew in small pieces, add the rest of the lemon juice and simmer for 15 minutes until the gravy is creamy. Remove any small bits of bone that come away easily serve in a hot dish, pouring the cream in at the last moment, and accompany with fluffy mashed potatoes to mop up the gravy.

CRUMBED VEAL STEAKS (serves 6)

6 thinly cut veal steaks	Salt and pepper
6 tablesp. fresh breadcrumbs	1 egg
2 tablesp. flour	2 tablesp. oil
50 g (2 oz) butter	1 lemon
Parsley for garnishing	

Place the veal steaks between two sheets of greaseproof paper and flatten them with a rolling pin or meat hammer until they are very thin. Cut each into halves, chill. Sprinkle with salt and freshly ground black pepper, dip into the flour, then into the beaten egg, and finally coat with breadcrumbs, patting them on with a palette knife. Lay flat and chill again for about half an hour. Heat the oil and butter together until moderately hot, fry the veal gently until golden brown on both sides, serve each garnished with a slice of lemon and a sprig of parsley. Delicately flavoured, these go well with grilled tomatoes, mushrooms fried in butter and fluffy mashed potato. Try cutting very thin slices from the top of a leg of mutton and preparing in exactly the same way. Delicious!

Mutton and Lamb

The flesh of mutton is a clear red in colour, lamb being a little paler, and the flesh of both should be firm and fairly dry to the touch, the fat should be waxy white. Mutton needs to be well hung, year old lambs (hoggets) for two or three days, and Spring lamb is eaten fresh; tell your butcher when you want to cook the joint to ensure it has been properly hung.

As the proportion of meat to bone is so high, the leg is the most economical joint for roasting, follow the directions given earlier in this chapter. With roast lamb or mutton it is traditional to serve Mint Sauce, but Onion Sauce or Red Currant Jelly are also pleasant accompaniments.

Mint Sauce

2 tablesp. finely chopped mint	1 dessertsp. sugar
4 tablesp. white wine vinegar	1 teasp. boiling water

Pour one teaspoon briskly boiling water over the chopped mint to bring out the flavour and set the green colour, add the sugar and vinegar, stir until the sugar is dissolved. Mint sauce should be made about 3 to 4 hours ahead to give time for the ingredients to combine well.

Onion Sauce

1 large onion	250 ml (½ pint) milk
25 g (1 oz) flour	50 g (2 oz) butter
A pinch of mace (optional)	Salt and pepper
1 tablesp. cream or top milk	

Peel the onion and cut into four, boil in a little salted water for 10 minutes, drain and chop finely. Simmer in half the butter until completely soft. Make a white sauce: melt the remaining butter in a small saucepan, stir in the flour, add milk by degrees stirring continuously over a low heat. Boil for 4 minutes until smooth and creamy, add the cooked onion and simmer again for 5 minutes. Then add one tablespoon of cream and a pinch of mace at the last moment, serve in a sauceboat.

BAKED LAMB WITH SAVOURY POTATOES
(serves 8)

1 leg of lamb about 2½ kg (5½ to 6 lb)	25 g (1 oz) butter
1 kg (2¼ lb) potatoes	Salt and pepper
4 tablesp. chopped parsley	1 clove garlic (optional)
300 ml (½ pint) chicken stock or a Knorr chicken cube and water	

Butter a medium sized meat tin, place a layer of thickly sliced potatoes on the bottom, sprinkle with salt and pepper and the chopped parsley. Pour the stock over the potatoes, arrange the leg of lamb on top. Melt the butter with the crushed clove of garlic, pour over the lamb, sprinkle with salt and bake in a moderately slow oven (170° C gas mark 3) for about 2¼ hours, cover with greaseproof paper if getting too brown. Test with a skewer, if the juice is colourless the lamb is done. Serve on a hot dish with the savoury potatoes, and young peas or carrots garnished with mint.

LAMB GRILLED ON SKEWERS (KEBABS)
(serves 6)

½ kg (1 lb) lean lamb, cut from the top of the leg
200 g (½ lb) button mushrooms
1 dessertsp. finely chopped onion
1 tablesp. lemon juice or vinegar

3 lamb kidneys
6 rashers streaky or flank bacon
Salt and pepper
2 tablesp. olive oil
6 metal skewers

Cut the lamb into 3 cm (1 inch) cubes; core the kidneys and cut each into 6 pieces, place in a small bowl with the meat, chopped onion, olive oil, lemon juice (or vinegar), and a good sprinkle of salt and freshly ground black pepper. Leave for about 2 hours or more, turning occasionally; cut each rasher into about 6 pieces.

Thread a mixture of pieces of lamb, kidney, bacon and mushrooms (if these are gently heated in a little butter first, they will not break) on the metal skewers, and place on the rack under a preheated grill. Cook for 5 minutes each side, brush with oil and grill a little longer if necessary, the lamb should be pinkish inside. Prawns, small cubes of lamb's liver or pieces of onion can also be included. Serve with rice. I always make a Tomato or Curry Dip to go with Kebabs.

Tomato Dip

1 onion
½ pkt. tomato soup mix
Chopped chives (optional)

25 g (1 oz) butter
1 cup water
½ teasp. sugar

Fry the finely chopped onion in the butter over low heat until golden, pour in the water mixed with the tomato soup, add the sugar and chives and simmer until slightly thickened (about 15 minutes).

Curry Dip

1 onion
1 dessertsp. curry powder
1 tablesp. cream or top milk

25 g (1 oz) butter
2 tablesp. flour
½ teasp. sugar

1 teasp. lemon juice	1 clove garlic
300 ml (½ pint) stock or	1 Knorr chicken cube and water

Fry the finely chopped onion in the butter until golden, sprinkle in the flour, sugar and curry powder, stir until blended. Add the stock, crushed garlic, lemon juice, and seasoning (not too much if you are using a stock cube as this is salty!), simmer for 15 minutes, stir in cream at the last moment.

Inexpensive Lamb or Mutton Dishes

SAUSAGE AND LIVER KEBABS (serves 6)

12 beef or pork sausages	6 rashers streaky or flank bacon
200 g (½ lb) sliced lambs liver	2 tablesp. flour
Salt and pepper	

Cut the liver into 3 cm (1 inch) squares, salt and pepper the pieces and dip into flour. Cut the sausages into four, and the rashers into six pieces. Thread a mixture of liver, bacon and sausage (pierce through the cut ends, not through the skin or it will break) onto metal skewers, and place on grill rack in pan under pre-heated grill. Cook for 5 minutes each side, brush with oil if the liver looks dry, and cook 2 minutes more if necessary. Serve with Tomato Dip (as above) and brown bread and butter. Especially popular with children!

STUFFED SHOULDER OF LAMB OR MUTTON
(serves 6)

1 shoulder of lamb or mutton about 1½ kg (2½ to 3 lb) in weight	25g (1 oz) butter
	Salt and black pepper
600 ml (1 pint) stock or water	2 tablesp.flour
	Juice of 1 orange (optional)

Ask the butcher to bone the shoulder, boil the bones for 2 hours in salted water, with sliced onion and some herbs to make the stock.

For Stuffing:

100 g (4 oz) fresh breadcrumbs	1 small onion
15 g (½ oz) butter	1 egg
1 dessertsp. chopped parsley	4 rashers streaky or flank bacon
½ teasp. chopped rosemary	

Make the Stuffing:

Cut the rashers into small pieces, fry in the butter with the chopped onion until golden, mix in the breadcrumbs, herbs, a little salt and pepper and the beaten egg. Spread this mixture on the meat, and roll into a neat shape, tying it with string in three places. Spread the 25 g (1 oz) butter over the meat, sprinkle with salt and black pepper and wrap in two thicknesses of greaseproof paper or one of foil. Place in a roasting tin with one cup of water and bake in a moderately hot oven (205° C gas mark 6) for about 2½ hours.

After 2 hours remove the wrapping and drain off every particle of fat, leaving the good meat juices in the tin, sprinkle in the flour, pour in the stock and mix well, scraping up the flavoursome sediment. Baste the meat with the stock, return to the oven and bake for the remaining 30 minutes, basting with orange juice added.

Serve on a hot dish with a little of the gravy poured over, and the rest served separately. Good with tomatoes, which may be peeled and baked whole in the meat dish with the joint for the last ten minutes; butter beans are a good alternative to potatoes.

Braised Neck of Mutton

Get the butcher to bone it and then follow the directions for braising given earlier in this chapter, adding onions, leeks, carrots, white turnips or swede, and celery. Neck of mutton is also good for stews.

Pork

The flesh should be faintly brownish pink, firm and fairly dry to the touch, with white fat and a smooth thin skin. Pork is usually in abundant supply in Winter, but does not keep well in hot weather – it should be eaten fresh and must always be thoroughly cooked.

The skin of joints for roasting should be scored by the

butcher, when cooked this makes the delicious crisp crackling. Pork is very rich and hard to digest, not the best choice for young children, the very old or invalids.

ROAST PORK

Spare rib which weighs about 1 kg (2 to 2½ lb) is best roast without wrapping in a preheated moderately hot oven (205° C gas mark 6) for about 1½ to 2 hours. The leg cuts are thicker; roast these wrapped in greaseproof paper or foil until 1 hour before the end of cooking time, then remove the coverings, for a 2 kg (4 to 4½ lb) joint allow 3 to 3½ hours.

To get crisp crackling: rub the scored skin well with salt before cooking, and 5 minutes before the end of cooking time, pour 2 to 3 tablespoons of boiling water over.

Roast Pork is usually served with forcemeat and apple sauce, apples may be baked in their skins with the joint, and can be used instead of apple sauce; purple sprouting broccoli or cabbage are good with pork.

Pork Forcemeat

25 g (1 oz) butter	1 medium onion
1 teacup fresh breadcrumbs	1 egg
1 tablesp. chopped sage or	1 dessertsp. dried sage
Salt and pepper	1 tablesp. dripping
A little milk	

Fry the finely chopped onion in the butter over low heat until golden, mix with the breadcrumbs, sage, seasoning and the beaten egg, adding a little milk if too dry. Heat the dripping in a small shallow tin, turn the forcemeat into it and pat out level, bake in the oven with the pork for 20 to 30 minutes until crisply browned, cut into squares to serve.

Apple Sauce

450 g (1 lb) cooking apples	2 tablesp. sugar
25 g (1 oz) butter	1 tablesp. water
Pinch of mace (optional)	

Put the apples, peeled, cored and sliced into a saucepan with

all the other ingredients, cover and stew slowly over low heat
until soft. Beat with a fork, or the handmixer, until smooth
and creamy, serve hot in a sauceboat.

LOIN OF PORK WITH VEGETABLES (serves 6)

About 1½ kg (3 lb) loin of pork	2 tablesp. dripping
8 to 10 potatoes	6 onions
4 large cooking apples	6 carrots
2 tablesp. chopped parsley	Salt and pepper
600 ml (1 pint) stock or water	

Ask the butcher to score the skin, and cut through the bones
for easy carving. Rub salt into the skin, place the joint in a
large roasting tin with two tablespoons hot dripping, and roast
in a preheated moderately hot oven (205° C gas mark 6) for
about 40 minutes, peel and quarter the potatoes, apples, onions
and carrots, pour the excess fat from the roasting tin, and
place the vegetables round the joint. Sprinkle with salt and
pepper, and chopped celery and parsley, and pour the stock
over. Continue to cook for another 1½ hours; cover with a
sheet of foil until ½ an hour before the end of cooking time, if
the meat is becoming too dry; continue to baste at intervals.
Five minutes before it is done, pour 2 to 3 tablespoons of
boiling water over the crackling to ensure crispness, serve the
joint separately from the vegetables to make carving easier.

CRUMBED PORK CHOPS (serves 6)

6 pork chops	3 tablesp. flour
1 large cup fresh breadcrumbs	1 egg
1 teasp. chopped sage	1 tablesp. cooking oil
1 teasp. grated orange peel	Salt and pepper
1 teasp. chopped parsley	Oil for frying

Accompaniment: two eating apples sliced and fried in butter
until golden.

Beat the egg with one tablespoon cooking oil, adding the
sage, parsley, finely grated orange peel, and salt and pepper.
Trim the excess fat from the chops, coat them in flour, dip
them in the herb-egg mixture and then into the breadcrumbs,
making sure that these will stick well by patting them down
firmly. Heat the cooking oil in a heavy frying pan, fry the

chops over a good heat for 5 to 7 minutes each side until the crumbs are crisp and brown, turn down heat and continue cooking until the meat is well done all through, turning very carefully so as not to break the coating. Serve with cauliflower or grilled tomatoes and mashed potatoes.

Inexpensive Pork Dishes

ROAST BELLY OF PORK (serves 6)

1½ kg (3 lb) pork belly	4 cooking apples
2 tablesp. dripping	Salt and pepper

Please do not be put off by the name, this cut of pork is delicious either hot or cold. The butcher will score the skin; rub well with salt, wrap in greaseproof paper or foil and place meat-side down on a wire rack in the roasting pan with hot dripping (placing the meat on the rack prevents absorption of extra fat). Roast in a preheated very moderate oven (180° C gas mark 4) for about an hour, remove wrapping and continue to cook for another ¾ to 1 hour basting every 15 to 20 minutes. Peel and core the apples and bake in the tin with the pork for the last half hour, basting at the same time as the pork. About 5 minutes before the end of cooking time, spoon 2 to 3 tablespoons of boiling water over the crackling to make it crisp. Place the meat and the apple on a hot dish, keep warm.

To make the gravy: pour off the fat, sprinkle in one tablespoon of flour, stir, scraping up the sediment and add 450 ml (¾ pint) stock or water, boil for a few minutes and strain into a gravyboat.

With such rich meat, plain baked potatoes in their jackets are a good idea; wash them, prick with a fork, rub a little butter into the skins (optional), and put into the oven for the last hour of cooking time. Turn occasionally, remove and keep hot when soft right through. Sweet-Sour cabbage (page 107), or buttered turnips go well with roast belly of pork.

Flank Bacon

Flank bacon and end pieces of bacon can be bought very cheaply, but as there is often a very low proportion of lean to fat, choose carefully. Try boiling a piece of flank bacon with an old fowl or very lean cut of topside of beef – it will add flavour and help to tenderize the meat. Thin slices of cheap bacon may be threaded between cubes of liver, kidney and mutton for Kebabs and will keep the meat succulent.

To find various other recipes for cooking meat, look in the Index under the headings: Beef, mutton, lamb, veal, pork and ham.

A Pressure cooker cuts cooking time and fuel costs when stewing or boiling meat – be sure to follow the manufacturer's instructions as to timing.

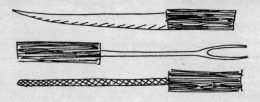

A LA MITCHELSTOWN

The finest tasting cheese dishes in Ireland are made from Cheddar and Gruyere, a la Mitchelstown. And to round off the meal – Irish Blue... just three of the great range of natural cheeses by Mitchelstown Creameries, Mitchelstown, Co. Cork.

Mitchelstown

MITCHELSTOWN CREAMERIES, MITCHELSTOWN, CO CORK

Quick and Easy Recipes

We live in the age of 'instant food' – tinned, dehydrated, frozen and packaged products of every description, a great boon to the busy housewife and career woman. These ready-made foods are often very appetizing but they are standardized – one tin of chicken soup tastes exactly like another beside it on the grocer's shelf. Unexpected combinations and flavours make them more individual: an added pat of butter, fresh ground black pepper, a dash of cream, a pinch of mace, fresh herbs or a spoonful of wine can make all the difference.

It is a good idea to keep a small store to fall back on in times of stress, but these foods tend to be expensive and they pall with constant repetition. There are the many simple homemade dishes using eggs, cheese, sausages, offal or leftovers which take very little time to prepare, and rice and various forms of pasta are quick and filling alternatives to potatoes.

Five Minute Soups

(1) *Baked Bean and Tomato Soup*: Heat a tin of tomato soup, add half a soup tin of water, 2 raw tomatoes peeled and chopped, and a small tin of baked beans. Stir continuously while heating to boiling point, add a little cream, garnish with chopped parsley and chives, and serve at once.

(2) *Cream of Celery-Chicken Liver-Soup:* Fry one or two chicken livers in butter for 3 to 4 minutes, season and chop very fine. Add to a tin of cream of celery soup and half a soup

tin of milk, heat together. Flavour with a few drops of Tobasco sauce and a squeeze of lemon juice, add a nut of butter or a dash of cream.

(3) *Shrimp and Sweetcorn Chowder*: Melt a nut of butter in a heavy saucepan, add 4 rashers of bacon cut into small pieces, fry for about 3 minutes. Add a tin of creamed sweetcorn, 600 ml (1 pint) of milk and a small tin of shrimps (discard the liquid). Heat gently, allow to simmer for 2 minutes, stir in 2 tablespoons of cream, dust with paprika and serve.

Fruity First Courses

(1) *Tomato Juice*: Mix a 560 g (19 oz) tin of tomato juice with the juice of half a lemon, a few drops of Tobasco sauce, 2 teaspoons very finely chopped raw onion and half a teaspoon Worcester sauce. Serve in small glasses very cold, with ice.

(2) *Grapefruit:* Cut in half across the sections, then using a small pointed knife, cut right round the grapefruit between the pith and the flesh – do not cut through the skin at the bottom. Now loosen the flesh of each segment by slipping the knife along each side of each membrane. Sprinkle with sugar, garnish with a glacé cherry in the centre, and a little chopped mint (optional), serve very cold in individual glass dishes, with more sugar separately.

(3) *Melon:* Be sure the melon is ripe, it should be slightly soft at the stem end and have a sweet fruity smell. Chill first, then cut a wedge for each person, scrape the seeds away, garnish with a slice of lemon, and hand sugar and ginger round separately.

(4) *Melon Balls*: cut the ripe melon in half, scrape out the seeds, then scoop out the soft flesh with a teaspoon and put in a bowl. Sprinkle with sugar to taste, and 1 tablespoon lemon juice, chill. It is delicious with a glass of champagne poured over instead of the lemon juice! Serve in individual glasses garnished with chopped crystallized ginger or a little chopped mint. Tinned grapefruit combines well with Melon Balls, garnish with chopped mint and serve cold.

Cold Starters

Most of the following take about ten minutes to prepare but
need to be made ahead and left to chill in a cool place unless a
refrigerator is specified.

(1) CHILLED CHEESE (serves 6)

90 g (3 oz) cream cheese
1 dessertsp. thick cream
30 g (1 oz) stale red Cheddar
   cheese
$\frac{1}{4}$ teasp. chopped parsley

90 g (3 oz) ripe Brie
1 teasp. port or sherry
Salt and pepper
1 clove garlic (optional)

Remove the Brie from its skin, add the cream cheese, port or
sherry, clove of garlic (if using it) and a pinch of salt and pepper.
Beat these well – the hand mixer comes in useful – then add the
cream and beat again. Turn onto a small dish, smooth into a
raised rounded shape with a knife, (or make individual
servings on coffee saucers) then chill in the frozen food com-
partment of the refrigerator. Just before serving, sprinkle with
very finely grated Cheddar cheese and the chopped parsley,
the combination of yellow, green and white looks very appetizing. Serve with thin slices of hot toast.

(2) LIVER SAUSAGE PATÉ (serves 6)

110 g (4 oz) liver sausage
2 teasp. port or brandy (optional)
1 dessertsp. thick cream

110 g (4 oz) cream cheese
2 teasp. chopped onion
Salt and pepper (freshly
   ground black pepper is best)

Scrape all the liver sausage from its skin into a small bowl,
chop the onion very finely, add with all the other ingredients
and mash well together, or use the hand mixer. Turn into a
small dish, and smooth the top; or shape into small pyramids
on coffee saucers for individual helpings, and leave to chill.
Serve with hot toast or Toast Melba: cut the crusts from very
thin slices of bread, then cut each slice into 4 squares. Place on
a wire cake rack and leave to toast in a medium oven (195° C
gas mark 5) until very crisp and golden brown – keep watching
as they burn quite suddenly! These can be kept in an airtight
tin for weeks.

(3) POTTED SALMON (serves 6)

A 99 g (3½ oz) tin of salmon	2 hard boiled eggs
50 g (2 oz) cream cheese	1 dessertsp. chopped parsley
2 teasp. chopped onion	Salt and pepper
1 lemon	2 teasp. capers

Put the salmon and all the juice from the tin into a bowl, flake
the fish, removing the small bones and skin. Mash the eggs,
add with the cream cheese, capers, chopped parsley, very finely
chopped onion, salt and if possible, freshly ground black
pepper, and mix well – the hand mixer is ideal. Turn into a
small dish and smooth the top or shape into rounded pyramids
on small individual coffee saucers. Chill and serve very cold,
with wedges of lemon and thin slices of brown bread and
butter.

Try the Chilled Cheese, Liver Sausage Paté or Potted Salmon
as sandwich fillings; on small crisp biscuits for cocktail snacks
or for light lunches with a salad of lettuce, tomato and hard
boiled egg.

Hot First Courses

(1) INDIVIDUAL BAKED EGGS

1 egg	1 tablesp. cream
1 tablesp. chopped ham	Salt and pepper
1 small nut of butter	Individual ovenproof dish

The ingredients are for one person. Butter a small ovenproof
dish (called a cocotte) for each person, put in a tablespoon of
chopped ham and break an egg into it. Top with a tablespoon
of cream, a nut of butter and season with salt and pepper.
Place the dish in a roasting pan half full of boiling water, and
bake in a moderate oven (195° C gas mark 5) for 7 to 9 minutes,
until the egg is set but not hard.

The chopped ham can be replaced with a tablespoon of
flaked salmon (tinned or fresh), grated cheese, cooked mushrooms, or sliced tomato.

(2) SCRAMBLED EGG RELISH (serves 6)

6 eggs	3 tablesp. cream or milk

60 g (2 oz) butter
Salt and pepper
Sprigs of parsley

3 teasp. Gentleman's Relish
6 squares of toast

Break the eggs into a bowl, add the cream or milk, salt and pepper (freshly ground is best) and beat with a fork until the yolks are well mixed with the egg whites. Melt the butter in a saucepan until just foaming, pour in the eggs and keep stirring over a moderate heat until the mixture thickens. Remove from the heat while the eggs are still soft and creamy, and spoon immediately onto hot buttered toast, lightly spread with Gentleman's Relish. Garnish with sprigs of parsley.

If using for a main course allow two eggs per person, and a whole slice of toast. A tablespoon of grated cheese, flaked tinned salmon or chopped parsley can be added to each serving.

(3) SARDINES ON FRIED BREAD (serves 6)

2 tins sardines
1 teasp. tomato puree
1 tablesp. cream
3 slices bread

2 hard boiled eggs
½ teasp. mustard
1 dessertsp. chopped chives

Drain the sardines, put into a small bowl with the rest of the ingredients except the bread. Mash well together, remove the crusts from the bread, cut the slices in half and fry in hot oil until crisp and golden. Drain the fried bread on kitchen paper, spread the sardine mixture, and heat under the grill or in the oven.

(4) MUSHROOMS ON TOAST (serves 6)

350 g (¾ lb) small mushrooms
25 g (1 oz) flour
2 tablesp. cream (optional)
6 small squares buttered toast

50 g (2 oz) butter
250 ml (½ pint) milk
Salt and pepper
Chopped chives

Wipe the mushrooms on a damp cloth, there is no need to peel them if they are fresh. Melt the butter in a small saucepan, add the whole mushroom caps and chopped stalks and fry for 2 to 3 minutes until golden. Set 6 mushrooms aside for garnishing, sprinkle the flour over the remaining mushrooms and add the milk. Season with salt and pepper, cook gently for another

3 to 4 minutes, stirring continuously, until the sauce has become creamy. Spoon onto the squares of buttered toast, top each with one of the reserved mushrooms and garnish with chopped chives.

To make this into a substantial lunch or supper dish, top each portion with two rashers of bacon fried and chopped, or a poached egg – or both!

(5) PRUNE AND BACON SAVOURY (serves 6)

6 cooked prunes	2 chicken livers
6 rashers streaky bacon	3 slices of bread

Wrap a stoned prune and a small piece of chicken liver in each thin slice of bacon (rinds removed, of course). Thread on a skewer and fry in butter, or bake in a hot oven until the bacon is crisp. Remove the skewer and place each 'Devil on horseback' as they are called, on a very crisp round of fried bread (cut into shape with a pastry cutter before frying).

Sardines of Fried Bread, Mushrooms on Toast, Scrambled Egg Relish, and Prune and Bacon Savoury can be used as a savoury finish to a meal.

Substantial Snacks (mostly inexpensive)

The following recipes involve very little preparation or washing up; fun too for teenagers to cook up for themselves.

(1) CHEESE AND HAM ROLLS (serves 6)

6 fresh white bread rolls	A little butter
2 tablesp. hot milk	100 g (4 oz) grated cheese
1 cup finely chopped ham	½ teasp. mustard (optional)

Cut the rolls in half lengthwise, pull out the soft white centres and put them in a small bowl. Add the chopped ham, grated cheese, mustard (if using it) and hot milk, mix all together. Fill the rolls with this mixture, secure the tops with wooden toothpicks, brush with melted butter and brown in a moderate oven (195° C gas mark 5) for 10 to 15 minutes until the cheese is melted, or heat under the grill.

(2) FRIED EGG SANDWICHES (serves 6)

6 eggs
12 slices of bread
Salt and pepper

100 g (4 oz) butter
3 tomatoes

Toast the bread lightly, butter each slice and keep warm. Fry
the eggs in butter, breaking the yolks so that they spread across
the egg whites. Fry until the yolks are just set, but not dry, lift
each egg onto a slice of toast. Slice half a tomato over each
egg, season with salt and pepper and top with another slice of
toast. Eat at once, hot and dripping with butter! ½ lb mushrooms fried with 6 rashers chopped bacon also make an
appetizing filling, as do ½ kg (1 lb) of hot fried sausages.

(3) CHEESY TOAST (serves 6)

6 slices of bread
6 rashers streaky bacon
Mustard

220 g (½ lb) cheddar cheese
50 g (2 oz) butter

Butter the bread, cut the cheese into very thin slices, or grate
it coarsely, and arrange it on the bread, spread on a little
mustard if liked. Top each slice with a rasher of bacon cut in
two, and grill, or toast in a hot oven, until the bacon is done
and the cheese is bubbling. A few slices of tomato can be used
as a topping instead of the bacon.

(4) FRIED SANDWICHES (one per person)

Make double decker sandwiches, using three thin slices of
bread for each, and the following fillings, secure with wooden
toothpicks.

(a) A slice of ham, spread with mustard (optional); and a
table spoon of grated cheese mixed with tomato sauce.

(b) Cold chicken, seasoned with salt and pepper; and thickly
spread liver sausage.

(c) A slice of cold beef, spread with horseradish sauce; and
two rashers of fried streaky bacon.

To make Fried Sandwiches: beat an egg into a cup of milk
and a tablespoon of flour, pour into a soup plate and dip each
side of the sandwich quickly into the batter, fry till golden on
each side. Alternatively brush the outside slices with melted
butter and bake in a moderately hot oven (205° C gas mark 6)

or under the grill, turning once, until crisp. Single decker sandwiches with a good flavoursome filling can also be fried.

Inexpensive Family Fillers

(1) MACARONI CHEESE (serves 4)

110 g (4 oz) cut macaroni	600 ml (1 pint) milk
50 g (2 oz) butter	50 g (2 oz) flour
150 g (6 oz) grated cheddar cheese	½ teasp. mustard (optional)
Salt and Cayenne pepper	2 tomatoes

Use cut macaroni (the pieces are about 3 cm (1 inch) long) or break long macaroni into short lengths. Bring plenty of water to the boil in a large saucepan, adding salt at the rate of one teaspoon to 1 litre (2 pints). Add the macaroni and cook uncovered until soft but not flabby (about 15 minutes). Drain, and add a nut of butter which will coat the pieces and stop them sticking together.

While the macaroni is boiling make the cheese sauce: melt the butter in a saucepan, mix in the flour, add the milk a little at a time stirring continuously with a wooden spoon to blend out the lumps, (the hand mixer will rescue it if it does go lumpy!). Cook gently for about 5 minutes until creamy, beat in two thirds of the grated cheese, add the mustard, salt and pepper to taste. Stir in the cooked macaroni, pour the mixture into a greased ovenproof dish, slice the skinned tomatoes over the top and sprinkle with the remaining cheese. Bake in a moderate oven (195° C gas mark 5) for about 25 minutes, serve. Suggested vegetables; peas, string beans or carrots.

(2) SPAGHETTI AND HASTY TOMATO SAUCE
(serves 6)

340 g (¾ lb) spaghetti	50 g (2 oz) butter
for the sauce:	1 large onion, chopped
25 g (1 oz) butter	3 large tomatoes
½ teasp. sugar	1 tablesp. chopped chives or parsley
1 tin cream of tomato soup	100 g (4 oz) grated parmesan cheese

Bring plenty of water to the boil in a large saucepan, adding one teaspoon of salt to every litre (2 pints) of water. Dip the ends of the long spaghetti, a handful at a time, into the boiling water, submerging it gently as it softens. Boil uncovered for 12 to 14 minutes until it is soft but not mushy. Drain, coat lightly with a little melted butter and place in a serving dish.

While the spaghetti cooks, make the sauce: heat the butter in a saucepan, add the finely chopped onion, fry till golden. Then put in the tomatoes, skinned and chopped, sugar and herbs and cook gently for about 5 minutes. Pour in the tomato soup and heat again. Pour the sauce over the cooked spaghetti, lifting it with two forks until all the strands are coated, sprinkle with grated parmesan cheese and serve.

The only way to cope with long strands of spaghetti is to spear a few with a fork, then twist it so that the spaghetti winds round the prongs forming a neat mouthful.

(3) SPAGHETTI WITH MINCED BEEF (serves 6)

340 g (¾ lb) spaghetti
2 tablesp. cooking oil
¾ kg (1¾ lb) minced lean beef
A little milk

25 g (1 oz) butter
370 g (13 oz) tin of tomatoes
1 thick slice of bread
1 clove garlic. 1 onion

Cook the spaghetti for about 14 minutes in plenty of fast boiling salted water, drain and put in a large serving dish with the butter melted over it – this will prevent it sticking together. Keep hot.

Soak the bread, crusts removed, in the milk until soft, mash with a fork and mix with the minced beef. Fry the chopped onion in the oil until golden, add the crushed garlic (if using), the peeled tomatoes with the juice from the tin, and the beef mixture. Stir well adding a little water if too dry. Simmer over a gentle heat for about 15 minutes, being careful not to cook too fast as the minced meat will become gritty (the bread soaked in milk also helps to keep the meat from turning into hard little pellets, always add it before cooking mince). Season with salt and pepper, and pour over the spaghetti. Cooked minced beef or mutton may be used instead of raw minced beef.

The spaghetti in the two fore-going recipes may be replaced by an equal weight of macaroni, pasta shells or noodles, bearing in mind that the thinner the pasta the less cooking it needs. Pasta is also very palatable served with stew instead of rice or potatoes, in this case coat the strands with butter and sprinkle with chopped fresh herbs and black pepper.

(4) MINCED BEEF WITH TOMATO AND BAKED BEANS OR CHILLI CON CARNE (serves 4-6)

750 g (1¾ lb) minced lean beef	2 tablesp. cooking oil
370 g (13 oz) tin of tomatoes	3 medium onions
430 g (15½ oz) tin of baked beans.	A little milk
1 thick slice of bread	Salt and pepper
2 tablesp. sultanas	¼ teasp. chilli sauce (optional)

Heat the cooking oil, add the chopped onions and fry until transparent. Soak the crustless bread until soft in the milk, mash and mix with the minced beef, add to the saucepan containing the fried onions. At the same time, add the peeled tomatoes with the juice from the tin, salt and pepper, sultanas and chili sauce, mix well and simmer very gently for 15 minutes, stirring occasionally. Finally mix in the baked beans, reheat and serve. You have now made Chilli con Carne, which sounds rather grand and tastes good! A variation of this is to add 3 cups of cooked rice in place of the baked beans, stir and heat, adding a little butter if too dry.

(5) FRIED SAVOURY RICE (serves 6)

340 g (¾ lb) Patna rice	Dripping or oil for frying
2 large onions	Salt and pepper
250 g (½ lb) mushrooms	2 tablesp. sultanas
1 dessertsp. chopped parsley	2 large tomatoes
6 rashers streaky bacon	1 egg per person

Cook the rice in boiling salted water for 14 minutes until soft to bite but not mushy. Strain and put under the hot tap to separate grains, drain well.

Heat a little dripping or oil in a saucepan, cut the rashers into pieces and fry, remove and keep hot. Slice the onions, fry till just transparent, add the mushrooms cut through caps and stalks, and fry for 2 minutes. Now add the sliced tomatoes, sultanas, and cooked bacon and simmer for another 5 minutes. Add the rice, mixing it in gently with a fork, and heat until the rice is really hot and has an attractive gloss from the fat, garnish with chopped parsley. Fry one egg for each person and place on top.

Alternatively, cooked meat or ham can be diced and heated, then added to the savoury rice. Good also with flaked tuna fish or salmon.

(6) CORNED BEEF HASH (serves 4)

440 g (15½ oz) tin corned beef
450 g (1 lb) cooked potatoes
2 tablesp. cream or milk

2 large onions
Salt and pepper
50 g (2 oz) butter

Melt the butter in a heavy frying pan, chop the onions finely and fry until golden. Dice the cooked potato, and the corned beef, mix together with the milk or cream and add to the fried onion. Stir gently with a fork, add salt and pepper to taste and cook over a very low heat for about 15 minutes. Good with boiled cabbage, and tomato ketchup. Left-over peas or carrots can be added with the potato.

A really substantial supper dish can be achieved by breaking an egg for each person into small hollows in the hash and placing the pan under the grill until the eggs are cooked.

(7) SPAGHETTI OMELET (serves 4)

440 g (15½ oz) tin Spaghetti in
tomato sauce
1 tablesp. chopped chives
2 tablesp. grated Parmesan cheese

6 eggs
1 tablesp. cooking oil
Salt and pepper

Beat the eggs until the whites and yolks are blended but not frothy. Rough chop the spaghetti, add to the beaten eggs with the chopped chives, salt and pepper. Heat the oil in a heavy frying pan, pour in the mixture and cook over low heat until set and lightly browned underneath. Slide carefully onto a hot plate, add a litte more butter to the pan, and turn the omelet over into the pan to cook the other side, or place the pan under the grill to cook the top. Sprinkle with grated Parmesan cheese, serve immediately.

(8) SPANISH POTATO OMELET (serves 4-6)

4 large boiled potatoes

1 large onion

8 eggs   Salt and pepper
50 g (2 oz) butter

Heat half the butter, fry the onion in it until golden. Cut the
boiled potatoes into dice, add with the rest of the butter to the
pan, and fry for a few minutes until really hot. Beat the eggs
with salt and pepper till the whites and yolks are well mixed
but not frothy, and pour over the potato onion mixture, cook
over low heat until browned underneath, and set. Slide
carefully onto a hot plate, add a little more butter to the pan,
and turn the omelet over into the frying pan to cook the other
side – or brown the top under the grill; serve cut into wedges.
Leftover cooked peas, carrots or cauliflower can be added with
the potato; or diced cooked ham.

(9) HARD BOILED EGGS WHITH CHEESE SAUCE
(serves 6)

6 hard boiled eggs   6 thick slices of bread
Fat for frying
For Cheese Sauce: 50 g (2 oz) butter
50 g (2 oz) flour   600 ml (1 pint) milk
75 g (3 oz) grated cheese   ½ teasp. mustard (optional)
Salt and pepper

Make the sauce first: melt the butter over a low heat, stir in
the flour, then slowly add the milk stirring all the time. Cook
over a low heat until thick and creamy (about 5 minutes), add
the cheese a little at a time, mustard, salt and pepper. Keep hot.

Cut the bread, crusts removed, into dice about 1½ cm (½ inch)
square and fry a few at a time in deep fat until very crisp and
golden. Drain on kitchen paper and put in a shallow dish. Cut
the hard boiled eggs in half lengthwise, place on the fried bread
cubes, pour the hot cheese sauce over. Serve at once, as the
fried bread will go soggy if not eaten immediately. A tin of
mushroom soup may be used instead of cheese sauce.

Meat Cooked in Minutes

Steak for frying and grilling is not cheap, but there is little
waste, it is quick to prepare and the flavour is delectable. The

undercut from the sirloin is the choicest and most expensive cut, but fillet of rump (frequently called chump in Ireland) is also a good buy. Ask your butcher for well hung steak, cut at least 2½ cm (1 inch) thick.

(1) FRIED UNDERCUT STEAK (EYE OF FILLET)
per person

1 piece of undercut steak	15 g (½ oz) butter
2½ cm (1 inch) thick	Salt and pepper
½ teasp. chopped parsley	A few drops lemon juice
½ slice crisply fried bread	

Suggested accompaniments: fried onions, mushrooms cooked in butter, grilled or raw tomatoes, left over potatoes fried up in butter, and mustard. Cook the vegetables you choose before the steak, as that must be eaten as soon as it is ready!

First prepare the parsley butter: mix a nut of butter for each person with half a teaspoon chopped parsley and a few drops of lemon juice, roll into small balls, or form into a small butter pat. Keep in a cool place.

Cut the surplus fat off the steak, flatten a little with a palette knife and brush with melted butter. Heat a heavy frying pan until really hot, grease by rubbing with a small piece of fat from the steak, place the steaks in the pan. Press down lightly with the palette knife, allow 2 minutes each side – the aim is to brown both sides to seal in the meat juices. Then lower the heat, and cook turning frequently for another 7 to 10 minutes for a medium rare steak, give about 4 minutes extra for well-done. Never use a fork for turning as if the steak is pricked the juices will escape.

When the steak is done, it should be dark brown outside, pink and succulent inside; if a really rare steak is wanted, cook over high heat for 4 to 5 minutes. Sprinkle both sides with salt and freshly ground black pepper and place each steak on a piece of crisp fried bread, pour over the gravy made like this: add half a cup well seasoned stock (water and a third of a Knorr beef cube will do) to the pan, scrape up the sediment from the meat; add a nut of butter and pour a little over each steak, garnish each with a parsley butter ball and serve immediately.

(2) GRILLED UNDERCUT STEAK

Turn the grill on full at least 10 minutes before you are ready to cook the steak. Prepare the steak as in the previous recipe place on the wire rack and grill for 2 minutes each side to seal in the juices, lower the heat, and continue cooking for another 7 to 10 minutes. Turn frequently and brush with melted butter, as it is apt to be drier and less juicy than fried steak. Sprinkle with salt, and pepper, garnish with parsley butter.

(3) MINUTE STEAKS

These are thin slices of the fillet, beaten until they are flattened. Suggested accompaniments: spinach or frozen peas, potato crisps – prepare these before you cook the steak.

Brush the steaks with oil or melted butter, season with salt and pepper, cook for one minute each side in a hot oiled frying pan. A dessertspoon of brandy may be poured over each steak just before removing it from the frying pan, scrape up the meat juices and pour them over the steak.

(4) FRIED RUMP FILLET STEAK

Allow 170 to 220 g (6 to 8 oz) per person. Take out of the refrigerator at least one hour before cooking. Trim off all excess fat, nick the edges to stop the meat curling up, and beat the meat with a heavy blunt object – there is a special meat tenderizing hammer, or use a wooden rolling pin! From here on the method is the same as for undercut steak, but allow 9 to 12 minutes cooking time after you have browned both sides; and omit the fried bread.

Accompaniments are similar too, but fried rump steak is also good with sweet corn, and fried eggs.

(5) HAMBURGERS (serves 4 to 6)

750 g (1¾ lb) lean minced steak   4 slices of bread
½ cup milk   1 large onion

2 eggs

½ teasp. Tabasco sauce (optional)

oil for cooking

3 teasp. salt

2 tablesp. flour

Soak the bread, crusts removed, in the milk until soft, mash with a fork. Skin and coarsely grate the onion. Mix the bread, onion, minced steak, salt, eggs and Tabasco sauce (if using) very lightly and quickly in a large bowl – handle the meat mixture as little as possible. Divide into equal portions and shape gently into round flat cakes with wet hands, coat with flour.

Heat a tablespoon of cooking oil in a heavy frying pan, and fry the hamburgers for about 3 minutes on each side. Reduce the heat and cook for about 8 minutes more, turning frequently. If the outside seems to be getting too hard, add 3 tablespoons of water half way through cooking time and cover pan. Alternatively, a tin of mushroom soup may be added instead of the water, this makes a delicious sauce. Hamburgers are good with fried onions, tomatoes or any green vegetable. They may also be served inside buttered buns, with mustard and tomato ketchup.

(6) LAMB CHOPS WITH SWEET CORN (serves 6)

6 chump chops (from the top of the leg)

480 g (1 lb) tin sweet corn

A little chopped rosemary, (optional)

1 medium onion

1 tablesp. cooking oil

2 medium tomatoes

Salt and pepper

Remove the fat from the chops. Heat the oil in a heavy frying pan, fry the chops over a good heat until brown on both sides. Add the grated onion, and peeled and sliced tomatoes, cook for another 2 minutes, lower the heat. Add the sweet corn, rosemary and salt and pepper to taste, cover closely, and simmer for 20 minutes, or until chops are tender.

(7) LAMB'S LIVER WITH BACON (serves 6)

750 g (1¾ lb) lamb's liver

1 tablesp. chopped chives and parsley

2 teasp. lemon juice

1 cup water or stock

12 rashers of bacon

90 g (3 oz) butter

2 tablesp. flour

Ask the butcher to slice the liver thinly. Heat a little of the butter in a heavy frying pan over medium heat, fry the bacon, remove from pan and keep warm. Dip the sliced liver in flour which has been seasoned with salt and pepper. Melt the remaining butter in the same frying pan, fry the liver gently for 2 to 3 minutes on each side – it should be soft and faintly pink inside. Keep hot. Add water or stock, lemon juice, 2 teasp. of flour and a little salt and herbs to the pan, stir and cook for about 5 minutes and pour over the lamb's liver. Goes well with instant mashed potato and frozen spinach, do not forget the mustard!

(8) LAMB'S KIDNEYS WITH TOMATO SAUCE
(serves 4 to 6)

6 lamb's kidneys
50 g (2 oz) butter
Salt and pepper
1 tablesp. sherry (optional)

1 tablesp. flour
2 tablesp. grated onion
½ tin cream of tomato soup

Skin the kidneys, cut in half lengthways and remove the white core, then cut into small pieces. Coat with seasoned flour, fry gently in the butter with the onion for about 6 minutes, add the tomato soup, cover and simmer for 5 or 6 minutes more over low heat. Delicious with noodles or rice.

Quick Chicken

For these quick methods of cooking chicken, buy a broiler, a young small bird about 1 kg (2½ lb) which will feed 3 to 4 people. If you are using a frozen chicken it must be completely defrosted before cooking; fresh chickens have a better taste and texture.

(1) CHICKEN WITH TOMATOES (serves 3 to 4)

1 kg (2½ lb) roasting chicken
1 tablesp. tomato ketchup
1 medium onion
3 rashers of bacon
½ a cup of chicken stock or
water with ½ Knorr chicken cube
1 tablesp. sherry (optional)
25 g (1 oz) butter

2 tablesp. cooking oil
1 tablesp. flour
4 large tomatoes
1 tablesp. sultanas

220 g (½ lb) macaroni shells

Cut the chicken into 5 neat joints: two legs and thighs, two wings with as much breast as possible, and the wishbone; strip any remaining meat from the carcase. Heat the oil in a heavy frying pan, fry the chicken until browned on all sides, remove and keep warm. Cut the bacon into small pieces, grate the onion and add to the pan, cook until done (about 4 to 5 minutes). Pour in the sherry (if using) simmer for 2 to 3 minutes then stir in the flour, seasoning, stocks, sultanas, tomato ketchup and the tomatoes peeled and chopped. Bring to the boil, return the chicken to the saucepan, cover closely and simmer over a medium to low heat for about 25 minutes.

While the chicken is simmering, cook the macaroni shells in plenty of boiling salted water for 16 to 20 minutes, drain and coat with butter. Serve the chicken on a bed of buttered macaroni shells.

(2) CURRIED CHICKEN (serves 3 to 4)

1 kg (2½ lb) roasting chicken
1 tablesp. cooking oil
1 tablesp. sultanas
1 dessertsp. curry powder
½ teasp. chilli sauce (optional)
300 ml (½ pint) stock; or water and ½ a Knorr chicken cube

1 medium onion
50 g (2 oz) butter
3 bacon rashers
1 clove garlic (optional)
1 dessertsp. flour
1 tablesp. cream

Cut the chicken carefully into 5 joints as given in the previous recipe. Fry them in the oil and half the butter until golden all over, keep hot. Add the remaining butter to the pan, fry the grated onion and rashers cut into strips for 4 to 5 minutes, put in the crushed garlic, sultanas and curry powder (freshly made is more aromatic), fry together for a minute or two then stir in the flour. Pour in the stock stir and bring to the boil, add the chicken, cover closely and simmer for about 20 to 25 minutes. Remove from heat, and stir in the cream; the chili sauce can be added if a hot curry is liked. Serve with rice, chutney and two freshly sliced bananas sprinkled with lemon juice and two sliced hard boiled eggs. Milk or cold beer are cooling drinks with a hot curry. Salted peanuts sprinkled over each serving add crunch!

Dehydrated, Tinned and Frozen Vegetables

There is no doubt that fresh vegetables in season, picked at the height of perfection, cooked with care and served with imagination form a delectable part of any meal. However, tinned, dehydrated and frozen vegetables are easily available time savers, and the flavour can be enhanced by tempting additions. Quality varies, especially in tinned vegetables, so choose carefully. Prepare frozen and dehydrated vegetables as directed on the packages, always keeping cooking time and amount of water added to the minimum, and drain well.

Seasoning and flavouring for vegetables (these apply to fresh as well).

(1) Butter is indispensable, it gives flavour and a delicious aroma to every kind of vegetable. Melt a little in a saucepan, heat until golden brown and pour over the dish, or place little pats here and there on top.

(2) Pour a little thick cream over peas, French beans, carrots, even cabbage, and season well.

(3) Rashers of bacon fried until crisp then broken into small pieces, make a good topping for Brussels sprouts, baked beans, cabbage, sweet corn and tinned tomatoes.

(4) Heat a clove of garlic, well crushed, with butter and pour over parsnips or tomatoes.

(5) Celery salt, a pinch of curry powder, or a few drops of Tabasco or chili sauce can be added to most vegetables.

(6) Fresh ground black pepper is preferable in most cases to ordinary white pepper. Paprika and Cayenne pepper make a good garnish for white vegetables like cauliflower, potatoes and parsnips.

(7) Onion or shallots chopped very finely and fried till golden in butter brings out the flavour of peas, carrots, French beans and baked beans.

(8) Chopped parsley and chives look fresh and inviting, and taste good with carrots, cauliflower, parsnips, potatoes and tomatoes.

(9) Fresh mint chopped and sprinkled over buttered carrots, or new potatoes smells delicious, or a sprig of mint may be added to the water in which peas, carrots or new potatoes are cooked.

(10) A little horseradish sauce mixed with cream or melted butter is piquant with peas, beans and cabbage.

(11) Grated cheese may be sprinkled over mashed potato, cauliflower, or tomatoes.

(12) A squeeze of lemon juice in melted butter is good with French beans or cauliflower.

(13) Half a teaspoon of sugar should be added to the water in which peas, carrots and French beans are boiled.

(14) A small pinch of mace, just enough to make people wonder what you have added, is good with cabbage, carrots or parsnips.

(15) Dehydrated vegetables can be improved by boiling them in well flavoured stock instead of water.

Swift Sweets

A bowl of fresh fruit or a choice of several kinds of cheese with biscuits makes a good finish to a meal, but those with a sweet tooth may enjoy the following.

(1) BANANAS AND CREAM

Slice or mash two bananas for each person (just when needed, or they will go brown), sprinkle with orange juice and serve with sugar and whipped cream.

(2) BANANA CUSTARD (serves 4)

600 ml (1 pint) milk
3 bananas
1 rounded tablesp. custard powder
3 rounded tablesp. sugar
½ teasp. cinnamon (optional)

Mix the custard powder with a little of the milk until it is a thin smooth paste. Add the cinnamon and the sugar to the rest of the milk in a saucepan, bring to the boil and as it foams up pour all together into the bowl with the custard. Stir until it thickens. Slice the bananas and mix into the hot custard, serve hot or cold.

(3) BAKED BANANAS (serves 4 to 6)

76 g (3 oz) brown sugar	6 bananas
300 ml (½ pint) orange juice	25 g (1 oz) butter
½ teasp. mixed spice	2 tablesp. sultanas
Grated rind of ½ an orange	3 tablesp. rum (optional)

Peel the bananas, cut in half lengthwise and place in a flat oven proof dish, previously buttered. Heat the orange juice, brown sugar, sultanas, grated rind of the orange, and butter all together until syrupy, pour over the bananas. Bake for about 15 minutes in a hot oven (220° C gas mark 7), serve hot. If you are using the rum, heat it, set alight and pour over the pudding at the table.

Hot Baked Bananas are delicious with vanilla ice cream.

(4) CHOCOLATE WHIP (serves 4 to 6)

220 g (8 oz) dark chocolate	5 eggs
4 tablesp. cream	

Break the chocolate into small pieces, heat gently with the cream in a small bowl over hot water until it melts, remove from heat. Separate the yolks from the egg whites, whip the whites until stiff enough to form peaks.

When the chocolate mixture has cooled a little, blend in the egg yolks, then fold in the whipped whites and spoon into individual glasses. Leave to set in the refrigerator, serve with whipped cream if liked. Chocolate Whip combines very well with stewed apples.

(5) ICE CREAM WITH HOT BUTTERSCOTCH SAUCE (serves 6)

Keep the ice cream in the freezer until needed, failing this, buy at the last moment and keep well wrapped in newspaper in a cool place.

1½ blocks Vanilla ice cream
For sauce:
120 g (4 oz) brown sugar
2 tablesp. golden syrup
6 tablesp. hot water

chopped walnuts

90 g (3 oz) butter
1 teasp. lemon juice

To make the sauce: melt the butter in a small saucepan, add the brown sugar, golden syrup and lemon juice, stir until the sugar is dissolved. Allow the mixture to boil for about 3 minutes, striring once, until it is golden brown. Now add the hot water, bring to the boil again and blend till smooth. Spoon the ice cream into individual glass dishes, garnish with chopped walnuts and hand round the hot sauce separately.

(6) ICE CREAM WITH HOT CHOCOLATE SAUCE
(serves 4)
1 block Vanilla or Polkadot ice cream
For Chocolate sauce:
220 g (8 oz) dark chocolate
1 teasp. brandy (optional)

3 tablesp. milk
1 tablesp. cream

Break the chocolate into small pieces, put with the milk in a small bowl over hot water. Stir occasionally until it melts, remove from heat and stir in the cream, and brandy if you are using it. Spoon the ice cream onto individual plates, hand round the Hot Chocolate sauce separately.

(7) WINDY PUDDING (serves 4)
1 pkt. strawberry jelly
450 ml (¾ pint) hot water

300 ml (½ pint) evaporated
milk or 300 ml (½ pint) cream

Dissolve the jelly in the boiling water, leave till cold but not set. Whip the cream (or evaporated milk) until stiff, fold gently into the jelly, making sure it is well blended.

Leave in a cool place to set.

(8) MELON GINGER (serves 4-6)
1 melon
1 Block Vanilla Ice Cream

1 Bottle Ginger Ale
25 g (1 oz) Crystallized Ginger

Cut a thin slice off one end of the whole melon, scoop out all the seeds, and fill melon with Ginger Ale. Stand upright in refrigerator, chill well. Serve with ice cream and chopped crystallized ginger having poured ginger ale.

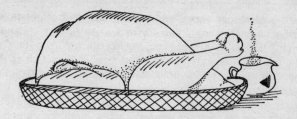

Poultry and Game

Chicken

In an age when the cost of living seems to go up almost every day, it is pleasant that due to mass production the price of chicken has dropped so that now, weight for weight, chicken is cheaper than sausages!

A bird weighing about 1 kg (2 to 2½ lb) is known as a broiler and will feed 4 people; a first year bird weighing over 1½ kg (3 lb) is called a roaster, and will feed 4 to 6; old hens are heavier and tougher, so must be boiled; they have excellent flavour. Frozen chickens should be allowed time to thaw naturally, and they take a little longer to cook; in my opinion fresh birds, if available, have a better taste and texture. There are more recipes for cooking chicken in other chapters, to find them look in the Index under 'chicken'.

BUTTERED ROAST CHICKEN (serves 4 to 6)

1 roasting chicken 1¼ to 1¾ kg (3 to 4 lb)
1 sprig parsley, thyme & tarragon
300 ml (½ pint) stock

50 g (2 oz) butter
1 slice lemon
1 dessertsp. flour
Salt and pepper

Boil the neck, gizzard and heart (but not the liver) in 300 ml (½ pint) water to make the stock. Rub half the butter into the skin of the chicken, sprinkle with salt; put the herbs and lemon into the bird with half the remaining butter (the rest is reserved for frying the liver). Place the chicken in a roasting tin, cover with greaseproof paper, and pour in a cupful of water (or half wine, half water). Roast for about 1 to 1¼ hours, basting 2 or 3 times, in a preheated moderately hot oven (205° C gas mark 6). Be careful not to overcook as this dries the meat; if the leg joints move easily when lifted and the juice runs colourless when the bird is pricked with a skewer, it is ready. Remove the chicken and keep hot, make the gravy in the roasting tin with the flour and stock, strain into a gravy-boat. Fry the liver in the last of the butter, slice and use for garnishing, with sprigs of parsley. Small sausages and bacon rolls (made by cutting streaky rashers in two, rolling them up and threading on a skewer) may be cooked in the tin with the chicken for the final 15 minutes, turning once, serve around the bird. Buttered Roast Chicken is very good cold.

GRILLED CHICKEN (serves 4)

If you are fortunate enough to have an electric grill with a rotary spit, use it for cooking small broiling chickens: brush the bird with melted butter, sprinkle with salt and pepper, and tie the wings and legs firmly with string. Impale it on the spit, grill for 45 minutes (the grill must be preheated) brushing once or twice with melted butter. The flavour has to be tasted to be believed!

CHICKEN WITH VEGETABLES (serves 4 to 6)

1 roasting chicken 1¼ to 1¾ kg (3 to 4 lb)	6 to 8 medium potatoes
	6 to 8 carrots
2 medium onions	4 sticks celery
2 tablesp. sultanas	25 g (1 oz) butter
100 g (¼ lb) flank bacon (optional)	25 g (1 oz) flour

Rub the chicken all over with a little of the butter, sprinkle with salt and pepper and place in the centre of a large roasting tin. Peel or scrape the vegetables, leave the potatoes whole, cut the onions and carrots into thick slices and dice the celery, arrange them all around the chicken. Cut the bacon (if using) into cubes and add with the sultanas; season, and pour in two cups of cold water. Cover the whole roasting tin with foil, turning it under along the edges to keep in the steam, put into a preheated moderately hot oven (205° C gas mark 6) and cook for about 1½ hours. When the chicken and vegetables are tender, remove and place the bird on a hot meat dish, and the bacon and vegetables together in another dish. Mix the remaining butter with the flour, divide into small pieces and stir into the stock in the roasting pan, adding more stock or water if necessary, boil up for about 3 minutes and pour into a gravyboat. A good family meal, and as it is all cooked together there is little washing up.

CHICKEN AND MUSHROOM CASSEROLE
(serves 4 to 6)

1 old fowl 1¾ to 2¼ kg (4 to 5 lb)	1 medium onion
Half a lemon	1 carrot
1 sprig parsley and thyme	1 cup milk
50 g (2 oz) flour	Salt and pepper
250 g (½ lb) mushrooms	50 g (2 oz) butter
8 rashers streaky bacon	2 tablesp. cooking oil
300 ml (½ pint) cream	Chopped parsley

Rub the bird all over with lemon, wrap in greaseproof paper and put it into a saucepan just large enough to hold it, with cold water to cover. Bring to the boil, skim, then add the sliced onion and carrot, the herbs and salt and pepper; squeeze the remaining juice from the lemon and add. Cover closely with greaseproof paper or foil as well as the lid and simmer over a very low heat until tender, about 2½ hours. (At this point the bird can be used as plain boiled chicken, either hot with parsley sauce or cold with salads and mayonnaise). To proceed with the recipe, skin the bird, cut into small joints and dip each piece into the milk and seasoned flour. Heat the butter and oil together in a heavy frying pan, put in the chicken joints and fry until golden, arrange in a deep casserole. Slice the mushrooms through cap and stalks, cut the bacon into strips and fry lightly together in the oil and butter and add to the casserole. Pour in two cups of chicken stock mixed with a dessertspoon of flour, and the cream, adjust seasoning, cover closely and cook in a very moderate oven (180° C gas mark 4) for about an hour. Bring to the table in the casserole, sprinkled with chopped parsley, it is very tender and succulent.

ECONOMICAL CHICKEN AND PORK BRAWN
(serves 4 to 6)

1 old fowl or large broiler	3 pig's feet (cruibíns)
Salt and black pepper	½ teasp. mace (optional)
1 sprig parsley and thyme	1 bayleaf

Clean the pig's feet, scraping away any discolouration. Put into a saucepan with the fowl, herbs, mace and seasoning, pour in cold water to cover, bring slowly to the boil and simmer closely covered for 4 hours. Lift out the fowl and pig's feet, and the herbs, and allow the stock to reduce considerably by boiling rapidly. Remove the skin from the bird, discard the bones, cut up all the pig and chicken meat finely and return to the stock to boil gently for 10 minutes. Strain the meat, put it into a pudding basin, press well down and add barely enough of the stock to cover the meat, leave in a cool place to set.

Duck

Choose a young duck with a flexible beak and legs, or better still, a plump duckling; old ducks are terribly tough and need very long slow stewing.

ROAST DUCKLING (serves 4)

1 duckling about 1½ kg (3½ lb) dressed weight	15 g (½ oz) butter
	1 clove garlic (optional)
For stuffing:	
1 tablesp. chopped mixed herbs or	1 teasp. mixed dried herbs
1 cup fresh breadcrumbs	1 medium onion
1 egg	Salt and pepper

Boil the giblets (neck, liver, heart and gizzard) for stock to make gravy. Rub the skin of the duck with a cut clove of garlic, and the butter, sprinkle with salt, if very fat, prick here and there with a fork, although personally I think it spoils the flavour to do this. Place on a rack in the roasting tin, pour in a cup of water and cook in a preheated moderate oven (195° C gas mark 5) until tender, about 1¼ hours, basting often and turning once. Remove and keep hot, pour off all the fat, then make a thin gravy with 1 dessertspoon flour to 450 ml (¾ pint) stock, scraping up all the sediment, and adding seasoning and the juice of an orange if liked. Roast duckling is perfect for a dinner party, with young new potatoes coated in butter and chopped mint, fresh green peas, and apple sauce. Allow 2 large ducklings for 6 to 8 people.

Rather larger first year ducks should be wrapped in greaseproof paper or foil, and cooked on a rack in a roasting tin in a moderately slow oven (170° C gas mark 3) for about 2 hours. Then remove the wrapping, raise the oven heat to moderately hot (205° C gas mark 6) and roast for another 30 minutes basting twice. Instead of basting with its own fat, try pouring off all the fat and using the juice from a small tin of pineapple pieces for basting; heat the pineapple pieces and serve on the dish around the duck.

ROAST GOOSE (serves 8)

1 young goose about 4½ kg (10 lb) dressed weight	15 g (½ oz) butter 1 dessertsp. flour
For stuffing:	
3 medium onions	50 g (2 oz) butter
3 cups mashed potato	Salt and pepper
1 dessertsp. chopped fresh sage	or 1 teasp. dried sage

Make the stuffing: chop the onion finely, frying in the butter until golden, add the mashed potato, sage and salt and pepper to taste, mix well. Stuff the goose with the mixture, covering the opening with a small piece of tinfoil, tie the wings and legs in position, prick the skin lightly 4 or 5 times with a fork, rub with butter and sprinkle with salt. Place on a wire rack in a roasting tin and cook in a preheated moderate oven (195° C gas mark 5) for about 2½ hours, covering with greaseproof paper or foil if getting too brown. As the goose is so rich, do not baste until halfway through cooking time; five minutes before dishing up, crisp the skin by spooning half a cup of boiling water over. Remove the goose and keep hot, pour off all the fat, add 1 tablespoon of flour and stir until browned, then add two cups of stock made from the giblets, season to taste and allow to boil for about 3 minutes before straining into a gravyboat.

Apple sauce is usually served with roast goose, but boiled sieved gooseberries are good too.

Duck or goose fat is very tasty for browning meat or onions before stewing, also delicious spread on toast if you have a good digestion!

Turkeys

Buy a hen turkey if possible, as these have more meat in proportion to bone than cock birds. Frozen turkeys need 1½ to 2 days to defrost, and on the whole are drier and less flavoursome than the freshly killed ones.

TURKEY COOKED IN A PARCEL

A turkey cooked in a parcel is moist and juicy; it needs no basting except for the last 30 minutes of cooking time. Prepare the stuffing the day before.

Rice and Bacon stuffing :

2 onions	25 g (1 oz) butter
The liver of turkey	100 g (4 oz) cooked rice
6 to 8 rashers of streaky bacon	1 tablesp. chopped parsley
50 g (2 oz) sultanas	1 egg

Fry the finely chopped onion with the bacon cut into small pieces in the butter until golden, add the chopped liver and cook for four minutes more. Mix in the rice, sultanas, chopped parsley and lightly beaten egg, season and allow to cool. Put the mixture into the turkey carcase.

Celery and Potato stuffing :

2 onions	25 g (1 oz) butter
½ cup chopped celery	1 cup mashed potato
½ teasp. mixed dried herbs	Salt and black pepper
2 tablesp. cream	

Fry the finely chopped onion and chopped celery in the butter until golden, mix in the mashed potato, herbs, seasoning and cream. Allow to cool, stuff under the skin in the area round the neck and top of the breast, and tie the opening in the skin firmly. Rub the turkey all over with butter, sprinkle with salt, and cover the breast with rashers of cheap flank bacon. Wrap the bird in 9 sheets of greaseproof paper, cook in a preheated moderate oven (195° C gas mark 5), timing according to weight.

Cooking times:
3 hours for a 4 kg (9 lb) turkey
4¼ hours for a 6¼ kg (14 lb) turkey
5 hours for a 8 kg (18 lb) turkey

About 25 minutes before the end of cooking time, remove the paper and bacon over the breast, baste the bird and sprinkle with salt, leave to brown in the oven. At the same time, put small sausages and bacon rolls in the oven to cook.

Accompany the turkey with all the delicious trimmings: bread sauce, gravy and Cranberry jelly, and braised celery (page 110) or Brussels sprouts with chestnuts.

BREAD SAUCE

Bread Sauce:

300 ml (½ pint) milk	1 small onion
3 cloves	A pinch of nutmeg
50 g (2 oz) soft breadcrumbs	15 g (½ oz) butter
½ teasp. salt	2 teasp. cream
A pinch of pepper	

Heat the milk and the whole onion with the 3 cloves stuck into it in a double boiler, or over very low heat for about 25 minutes. Stir in the breadcrumbs, salt, pepper and nutmeg, simmer gently for another 25 minutes. Remove the onion, add the butter and cream, beat well with a fork, serve hot.

Now-a-days, turkeys are available throughout the year, if cooking a small bird, bake it wrapped in a parcel or proceed as for Buttered Roast Chicken (page 76), allowing 15 minutes to ½ kg (1 lb) plus 15 minutes added at the end. It will take a little less time to cook if not stuffed.

STEWED PIGEONS (serves 4)

Pigeons may be cooked very fresh, on the day of killing; or after hanging for 4 days

4 pigeons	50 g (2 oz) butter
450 ml (¾ pint) stock or water	2 medium onions
3 tablesp. seedless raisins	1 tablesp. flour
Salt and pepper	

If there is no one to pluck the pigeons for me, I save time by cutting off the wings and removing the skin from the carcase, the feathers and all. Brown the prepared pigeons all over in butter over medium heat, remove and keep hot, fry the onions in the butter until golden. Put the birds back into the saucepan with the onions and add the stock or water, washed raisins and seasoning and simmer closely covered over very low heat for about 2½ hours; or bake in a covered casserole in a very moderate oven (180° C gas mark 4) for the same time. When tender, cut the pigeons in half and serve on a bed of boiled rice. Thicken the gravy with the flour, and serve separately. Vegetables such as diced celery or sliced carrots may be added half way through cooking time with a little more liquid; or 2 tablespoons of tomato purée gives added flavour.

PHEASANT CASSEROLE (serves 3 to 4)

Roast pheasant is always rather dry, I prefer to cook it in the same manner as for Stewed Pigeons, (previous recipe). Replace the 4 pigeons with a pheasant, which should have been hung for about 7 days. After browning place the bird, breast side up in the saucepan or casserole, and cover with rashers of fatty bacon, add the ingredients as for Stewed Pigeon, and simmer closely covered for about 1½ hours, serve with fluffy mashed potatoes, garnished with mushrooms.

RICH RABBIT STEW (serves 3 to 4)

1 young rabbit	50 g (2 oz) butter
100g (¼lb) streaky or flank bacon	4 carrots
300 ml (½ pint) stock or water	2 onions

A sprig parsley, thyme &
   rosemary
A pinch of mace

2 white turnips
1 clove garlic (optional)
Salt and pepper

Rabbit should be drawn immediately and hung for about 3 days.

Cut the rabbit into joints, and as there is a good amount of meat along the backbone, divide this into two or three pieces; wash under cold water and dry. Melt the butter in a saucepan, fry the chopped onion and the bacon cut into small cubes until golden, lift out and keep hot. Fry the rabbit pieces gently on both sides, sprinkle the flour in and continue frying for 5 minutes. Put back the onion and bacon, add sliced carrot and turnip, the herbs, mace and crushed garlic (if using). Season and cover closely, stew over gentle heat or in a very moderate oven (180° C gas mark 4) for about an hour or until the rabbit is tender. Serve the rabbit surrounded by bacon and vegetables, with the sauce poured over, and lots of floury boiled potatoes to mop up the gravy.

CURRIED RABBIT

Exactly the same as previous recipe, but add 1½ dessertspoons of fresh curry powder while frying the rabbit pieces, a tablespoon sultanas and a teaspoon of lemon juice with stock. Chili sauce may be cautiously added to make the curry hotter; serve with boiled rice, chutney, sliced hard boiled eggs, sliced banana and 2 tablespoons of dessicated coconut soaked in a cup of milk.

SNIPE AND WOODCOCK

Snipe and woodcock are prepared and cooked in the same way. Allow one snipe or one woodcock to each person, they should be hung for about 4 days before cooking. Cook without drawing (that is, with the insides in!), skin the head and push the beak through the legs and body to hold them in position, (this looks very neat, but when I am in a hurry, I'm afraid I cut off the head and wings, there is no meat on them, and tie the legs together). Brush the birds with melted butter, sprinkle

with salt, cover the breast with streaky rashers and lay each
bird on a piece of toast to catch the juices. Roast for about 15
to 20 minutes in a moderate oven (195° C gas mark 5) brushing
frequently with melted butter. Many people prefer snipe and
woodcock under-done, if so, cut the cooking time by a few
minutes.

ROAST WILD DUCK (serves 4)

2 wild duck   50 g (2 oz) butter
4 thin slices fried bread   2 oranges
1 teasp. olive oil   ½ teasp. sugar
300 ml (½ pint) gravy   Salt and pepper

Hang the ducks for three days, then pluck, draw (remove the
insides) and tie for roasting. Brush well with melted butter,
sprinkle with salt, and roast in a moderate oven (195° C gas
mark 5) for 45 minutes, or less if liked under-done. Brush
frequently with melted butter, and cover with buttered paper
if getting too dry. When ready to serve, split each bird in half,
and serve cut side down on a piece of crisply fried bread,
garnish with sprigs of parsley. Peel and slice the oranges,
discarding all the white pith, sprinkle with a little oil and
sugar, arrange around the serving dish.

To make the gravy: sprinkle one tablespoon of flour into the
roasting pan, scraping up the encrusted juices, add 300 ml
(½ pint) good stock, and the juice of one orange or a glass of
port, or both, boil for 3 minutes and strain into a gravyboat.

Cooking with an Irish Flavour

Many Irish Traditional dishes have the most delightful and
melodious names: who would ever guess that Cruibins are pig's
feet, or that Drisheen is a type of sausage made of sheep's
blood, mutton suet and oatmeal. The delicate-sounding
Colcannon is a mixture of mashed potato, boiled green cabbage,
onion and butter; Champ is even more down-to-earth:
mashed potato and scallions (spring onions) browned in the
oven!

In addition to traditional fare, there is a wide range of Irish-
made foods which can be used to impart a distinctive flavour
to your cooking: beautiful Irish hams, very pink and tender;
prepacked rashers and small joints of boiling bacon which have
a pleasant smoky taste; and a wide range of cheeses. Guinness
and Irish whiskey too!

IRISH TURNIP SOUP
(TRADITIONAL) (Serves 6)

I think this must be a traditional recipe, as an old Kerry
woman, a friend of mine who lives near Castle Cove, taught
me how to make it. She cooked it in a bastable, which is a
three-legged iron pot with a lid and a handle by which it can
be suspended over the fire, commonly used in every household
in times gone by. It could be used for soups, stews, rich brown
pot roasts and delicious brown or white 'cakes'; my old friend
told me that her mother had also used hers for roast goose and
'the grandest fruit cake you ever saw' at Christmas.

3 large white turnips or	1 large swede
1 large onion	600 ml (1 pint) milk (2½c)
900 ml (1½ pint) chicken stock or	2 Knorr chicken cubes and water
50 g (2 oz) butter	
25 g (1 oz) flour	salt and pepper
3 cloves	1 teasp. sugar

Peel and chop the turnips and onion, add to melted butter in a heavy saucepan, cover closely and cook gently for about 20 minutes. Now pour the stock over, add 3 cloves and simmer together for 30 minutes, or until turnip is tender, then discard the cloves. Rub through a sieve or liquidize and return to pan. Mix the flour to a smooth paste with a little of the milk, add this to the soup with the rest of the milk and sugar. Season to taste and cook for 10 minutes. Unusual and very good, especially if a liquidizer is used.

IRISH POTATO SOUP (TRADITIONAL) (serves 6)

5 big potatoes	2 large onions
75 g (3 oz) butter	Salt and pepper
1 sprig parsley, thyme and sage	or ½ teasp. mixed dried herbs
1¼ l (2 pints) water	300 ml (½ pint) milk
Chopped chives or chopped mint	2 tablesp. cream or 'top milk'

Peel potatoes and onions, slice thinly and simmer slowly in butter, closely covered, for 15 minutes, do not brown. Add water and herbs, salt and pepper and continue on low heat until vegetables are tender, about 25 minutes. Discard sprigs of parsley, thyme and sage, beat for 5 minutes with a fork, add the milk, bring back to boil and serve piping hot with cream and chopped chives, or mint. To make this soup really smooth and creamy, sieve it, or put it through the blender before adding the cream and chives. This gives it a lovely texture, but it is not strictly as our grandmothers made it.

BACON AND CABBAGE BROTH
(TRADITIONAL) (serves 4-6)

250 g (8 oz) streaky bacon	1¼ l (2 pints) cold water
½ cabbage	1 large onion
½ a swede turnip	Salt and pepper

110 g (¼ lb) dried peas soaked or overnight
6 slices of toast

250 g (½ lb) fresh or frozen peas
1 large carrot

Dice bacon into medium sized pieces, and put into water plus the previously soaked dried peas, if you are using them. Simmer for 1½ hours, skim off all scum and fat. Shred the cabbage, slice the carrot, turnip and onion, add to saucepan, with fresh or frozen peas (if no dried peas are used). Simmer for 45 more minutes. Place a crisply toasted slice of bread into each soup plate, and pour hot soup over. Very good.

IRISH STEW (TRADITIONAL) (serves 4)

1 kg (2 lb) gigot chops (these come from the sheep's shoulder) or neck of mutton
Salt and pepper

6 medium onions
1 kg (2 lb) potatoes
600 ml (1 pint) water
Chopped parsley

Skin the onions, wash and peel the potatoes. Cut the meat into neat pieces, being careful to remove skin, fat and bone splinters. Season with salt and pepper, place in a stewpan and cover with one onion finely chopped and one sliced potato – these boil down to thicken the gravy. Add the water, cover closely with foil and a lid and simmer over gentle heat or in a very moderate oven (175° C gas mark 3) for an hour. Now add the remaining onions and potatoes whole, simmer again for one hour until the vegetables are cooked – the meat should be so tender that most of the bones are easily removed as you dish up. Serve very hot, garnished with parsley.

The purists will tell you that this is the only way to make Irish Stew, but I break with tradition and make mine like this:

CAREYSVILLE IRISH STEW (serves 4)

1 kg (2 lb) gigot chops
6 medium carrots
1 dessertsp. flour
chopped chives and parsley

2 medium onions
300 ml (½ pint) water
Salt and pepper
1 clove garlic (optional)

Cut the meat into pieces, removing skin, fat and bone splinters, coat each cutlet with flour and season with salt and pepper.

Simmer with chopped onions and water for one hour, add the carrots, each cut into about four large pieces, the garlic, and a little more water if it is too dry, and simmer again for about 45 minutes. Remove the bones as you dish up, and garnish with chopped chives and parsley. Have ready lots of snowy mashed potato to mop up the delicious meaty gravy.

STEAK STEWED WITH GUINNESS (serves 4-6)

1 kg (2 lb) stewing steak	5 onions
1 tablesp. flour	300 ml (½ pint) Guinness
1 teasp. brown sugar	8 bacon rashers
1 tablesp. raisins (optional)	75 g (3 oz) lard
salt and pepper	Chopped parsley

Cut the steak into bite sized cubes, roll in seasoned flour and brown in the lard with the chopped bacon. Place the meat in a stewpan or deep casserole, peel and chop the onions and fry till golden before adding them to the meat. Add the raisins and brown sugar, pour in the Guinness, cover closely and simmer over a low heat or in a very moderate oven (175° C gas mark 3) for about 2½ hours. Stir occasionally, and add a little more Guinness or water if the rich brown gravy gets too thick. Serve with boiled potatoes or rice. This is a good standby if you have weekend visitors, as it can be made a day or two ahead and reheated when needed; Careysville Irish Stew also has this advantage.

PORK STEAKS COOKED IN BUTTER (serves 3-4)

2 pork steaks	100 g (¼ lb) butter
2 cups fresh white breadcrumbs	1 egg
2 tablesp. flour	4 tablesp. cooking oil
2 dessert apples	1 lemon
Parsley sprigs for garnish	Salt and pepper

Remove all the fat and stringy bits, cut the steaks across the length into round medallions about 1½ cm (½ inch) thick, flatten slightly with a pallette knife. Beat up 1 tablesp. of the oil with the egg until well mixed but not frothy, roll the pork medallions in well seasoned flour, dip into the beaten egg mixture and coat with breadcrumbs, patting them down with the palette knife so that they stick on well. Now heat half the butter and ½ the remaining oil in a frying pan until hot but not browned, lower the heat and cook the medallions a few at a time for about 8 minutes on each side – the oil mixed with the egg and breadcrumbs gives a very crisp finish. Add more butter and oil as needed to cook the remaining meat, keep hot in the oven. Core the apples and cut each into about five rings, leaving the skin on, fry gently in butter until golden brown and soft. Arrange the pork medallions on a large oval dish surrounded with apple slices and lemon wedges, and garnished with parsley. Serve with fluffy mashed potatoes and a green vegetable. Apple sauce (page 50) can be used instead of fried apple slices.

This is my own recipe, and the contrast of crisp coating with the tender succulent pork is delicious. Pork steaks can also be stuffed with a mixture of herbs, onion, egg and breadcrumbs, and braised in the oven in a covered casserole for 1½ hours. Add a little stock or water, and a tablespoon of sherry after an hour's cooking. Another recipe for pork steak is in the chapter on Entertaining: Pork Steaks with Mushrooms and Cream Sauce.

BLACK PUDDING (TRADITIONAL)

Black pudding is good in a mixed grill with any of the follow-ing: chops, sheep's kidneys, sausages, rashers, tomatoes and mushrooms; or with bacon and egg and fried bread for break-fast. Children sometimes find it rather highly flavoured; try it fried and mixed with sliced tomato as a filling for omelets: the bland taste of the egg makes a good foil, as does mashed potato. Black pudding is a cheap and excellent source of iron in the diet.

To cook Black Pudding: cut into slices 1½ cm (½ inch) thick, remove skin and fry over medium heat for 4-5 minutes, turning once, drain on kitchen paper, and serve.

DRISHEEN (TRADITIONAL)

Drisheen which looks like a white 'black pudding', is also a healthy addition to the diet and is gently poached for about 20 minutes in milk or water, or a mixture of both, then split open and eaten with butter, salt and pepper; alternatively it may be poached, then sliced and served in white sauce to which chopped parsley and a little mace is added.

Irish Hams

A whole ham, cooked on the bone, is a most wonderful stand by when one has a houseful of people to feed for some special family gathering, with a succession of meals to plan. It is more economical to buy a full ham of about 5 to 6½ kg (11 to 14 lb) as the small ones are apt to shrink a bit when cooking. Cook the ham at least two days ahead and leave it to 'set' in a cool place, as this makes it easier to carve into beautifully thin slices.

BOILED HAM, SERVED COLD

Soak the ham for 12 hours in cold water. Wrap it in several sheets of greaseproof paper, place in a ham kettle or large preserving pan. Cover with cold water, bring slowly to the boil and start timing when the water starts to bubble gently. The ham will shrink and be apt to break if boiled too rapidly, keep the heat low. Allow the following cooking times.

3 hours for 3 kg (6 to 7 lb)
3¾ hours for 4 kg (9 lb)
4½ hours for 6½ kg (14 lb)

Allow the ham to cool slightly in the water, then lift out and drain well. The skin should come away easily, leaving a smooth surface for the finish of your choice, there are several ways to do this.

(1) Mix 1 tablespoon dry mustard with 2 tablespoons brown sugar and one tablespoon vinegar. Place the cooked ham in a

roasting tin, spread with the mixture, and brown in a fairly hot oven (205° C gas mark 6) for about 20 minutes until it is a shiny chestnut colour. Leave in a cold place to set.

(2) Score the fat of the cooked ham in a criss cross pattern, stick a clove into the centre of each square, then spread with a mixture of 3 tablespoons brown sugar and 1 tablespoon Guinness or pineapple juice. Brown in the oven for 20 minutes. Leave in a cool place to set.

(3) Reduce 5 slices of very crisp toast into crumbs with a rolling pin, sprinkle over the ham and garnish with parsley. Leave in a cool place to set.

BAKED HAM

If you have no container large enough to boil your ham, soak it for 24 hours in several changes of cold water, dry it and cut away any discoloured fat. Cover with a layer 1½ cm (½ inch) thick of paste made with flour and water. Bake in a moderate oven (195° C gas mark 5) following the same time for weight as for boiled ham, cover with greaseproof paper if necessary.

TO USE LEFTOVER HAM

For all the following recipes, keep in mind that the ham is salty to start with, season with caution! Recipes serve 4-6.

(1) *Ham and Egg Supper dish*: Mix 2 cups of ham cut into cubes with 4 roughly chopped hard boiled eggs in a shallow ovenproof dish. Make 600 ml (1 pint) creamy white sauce, pour over, cover top with breadcrumbs and grated cheese. Heat in the oven or under the grill until nicely browned and piping hot. Serve with rice or mashed potatoes.

(2) *Creamed Ham*: Combine the contents of a tin of condensed mushroom soup, 3 cups of minced ham and half a cup of fried onion in a shallow ovenproof dish. Bake in a very moderate oven (180° C gas mark 4) for 15 minutes. 600 ml (1 pint) white sauce can be used instead of mushroom soup, and 2 tablespoons of Sherry is a pleasant addition. This mixture also makes a good filling for pancakes, omelets, small savoury tartlets or a pastry flan case.

(3) *Savoury Spaghetti with Eggs*: Heat the contents of a tin of spaghetti in tomato sauce, cover with a layer of half a cup fried onion and half a cup of chopped ham. Poach 4 eggs until just set, place on top, sprinkle with grated cheese and brown under the grill.

(4) *Savoury Rice with Ham:* Fry 1 large chopped onion in 2 tablespoons cooking oil until golden, add 2 cups cooked rice, 2 tablespoons sultanas, 1 cup chopped ham and 2 tomatoes peeled and sliced. Mix gently and cook until heated right through. A clove of garlic crushed and added with the onion, is delicious; and chutney is a good accompaniment.

(5) *Ham Fingers:* Mix 4 tablespoons minced ham with 2 tablespoons thick cream or cream cheese and 2 tablespoons chutney. Spread thickly on fingers of very crisp fried bread, heat under the grill and serve piping hot. A good first or last course.

(6) *Suprise Baked Potatoes:* Bake the potatoes in their jackets, cut the top off the potato, scoop out and mash with butter, a little milk, salt and pepper, and some chopped ham. Fill the skins with the mixture, place a small nut of butter on top of each and reheat before serving.

(7) Small quantities of cooked ham can be beaten in with the eggs for ham omelets, fried with mushrooms and served on toast, or used for stuffing tomatoes.

HOT BAKED HAM OR BACON (serves 6-8)

Soak a piece of gammon or collar bacon 1½ kg (3 to 4 lb) in weight, in cold water for about 6 hours. Place in a roasting tin, fat side up, cover with tinfoil and bake in a very moderate oven (180° C gas mark 4) for 35 minutes to each half a kg (1 lb). About 40 minutes before it is due to come out of the oven, remove the skin carefully, sprinkle 25 g (1 oz) fresh breadcrumbs mixed with 2 tablespoons of brown sugar and put back for the remaining cooking time.

Alternatively, having stripped off the skin, baste the ham at frequent intervals with one of the following mixtures.

(1) Heat the juice of two oranges with 3 tablespoons of brown sugar and a pinch of mace (optional) until the sugar is

dissolved, pour over gammon and baste frequently, serve hot with potatoes and a green vegetable.

(2) Dissolve two tablespoons brown sugar in 150 ml (¼ pint) of Guinness, the juice of half a lemon and half a teaspoon cinnamon and baste frequently.

(3) Sprinkle gammon with one teaspoon dry mustard and two tablespoons sugar, baste with juice from a small tin of pineapple; heat the pineapple and serve with the gammon.

BOILED PIG'S HEAD (TRADITIONAL)

½ a salted pig's head
1 large cabbage
1 large onion
Parsley Sauce:
25 g (1 oz) butter
250 ml (½ pint) milk
2 tablesp. chopped parsley

1 carrot
1 white turnip

25 g (1 oz) flour
Salt and pepper
½ teasp. mace

Clean the head carefully in water, scraping away any rusty areas. Soak for 6 to 8 hours, place in a large saucepan covered with cold water and bring slowly to the boil. Simmer for 2½ hours adding prepared root vegetables one hour before end of cooking-time. Make the parsley sauce: melt the butter in a small saucepan, stir in the flour, then add the milk slowly stirring continuously over low heat until the sauce is creamy (about 4 minutes) add the chopped parsley and mace, keep hot. Also cook the cabbage in a little briskly boiling salted water with the lid off for about 10 minutes, drain well.

Remove the skin from the cheek and tongue, and any bones which will come away easily. Serve on a large dish, surrounded by the root vegetables and the cabbage. Accompany with floury potatoes boiled in their skins, and the parsley sauce. Salted pig's head in the shop looks rather macabre, but cooked like this it is quite surprisingly palatable, and it is not expensive.

Dublin Bay Prawns

These are often bought ready cooked from the fishmonger. If you are lucky enough to get them straight from the sea, plunge them into boiling salted water (just enough to cover, or you will loose much of the flavour) and simmer for about 5 to 7 minutes. Cool in the water, remove shells and any black veining. Lovely cold, served with salads, mayonnaise, brown bread and butter and garnished with lemon.

All shellfish must be eaten very fresh.

DUBLIN BAY PRAWNS WITH YELLOW RICE
(serves 4)

½ kg (1 lb) shelled prawns
1 clove garlic
220 g (½lb) patna rice
½ teasp. turmeric
a little flour

50 g (2 oz) butter
1 tablesp. sultanas
1 lemon
Parsley for garnishing
Salt and pepper

Cook the rice in rapidly boiling salted water, with the sultanas and turmeric (this gives the rice the rich yellow colour) for about 14 minutes until soft to bite. Put the rice in a sieve, and run hot water over, drain well and keep hot in the warming oven. Heat the butter, with the crushed garlic if you are using it, in a frying pan until melted. Roll the prawns in the flour mixed with salt and pepper, then cook for about 4 minutes in the butter till thoroughly hot, place in the centre of a large dish surrounded by yellow rice, and pour the butter over. Garnish with wedges of lemon and sprigs of parsley, serve with grilled tomatoes, or peas, and Fresh Tomato Sauce, (page 29) or Hollandaise Sauce (page 103)

PRAWNS WITH MUSHROOMS (serves 4)

½ kg (1 lb) cooked shelled prawns
250 g (½ lb) mushrooms
250 ml (½ pint) light cream or milk
2 teasp. Irish Whiskey

50 g (2 oz) butter
25 g (1 oz) flour
Salt and pepper

Melt the butter in a saucepan, fry the sliced mushrooms, stalks too, for a few minutes until soft, remove and keep hot. Blend the flour into the butter remaining in the saucepan, pour in the light cream or milk, season and stir continuously over low heat until creamy. Sprinkle the Irish Whiskey over the prawns, add them and the mushrooms to the contents of the saucepan and heat. Serve with boiled rice.

DUBLIN BAY PRAWNS GRILLED

½ kg (1 lb) cooked shelled prawns   50 g (2 oz) butter
1 clove garlic (optional)   Salt and pepper
1 lemon

Melt the butter with the crushed garlic if you are using it.
Place the cooked shelled prawns on foil in the grill pan, season
with salt and pepper (black pepper from the pepper mill is
nicest) brush with melted butter and grill for about 5 minutes,
brushing with the butter frequently, and turning over once.
Serve on a hot dish with remaining butter poured over,
garnished with lemon wedges and accompanied by savoury
rice made like this: fry one small onion, cut up finely, in 25 g
(1 oz) butter until transparent, add 2 teaspoons tomato puree
and 2 cups cooked rice and heat, stirring with a fork until
really hot. All the recipes given for prawns are equally good
for shrimps.

BOXTY (TRADITIONAL)

450 g (1 lb) potatoes   100 g (4 oz) flour
1 egg   1 teasp. salt
½ teasp. baking powder   a little milk

Peel the potatoes, boil half until soft, then mash them. Mean-
while grate the remaining half of the potatoes. Mix the mashed
potato, raw grated potato, sifted flour, salt and baking powder
into a soft dough with the egg and a little milk if needed. Drop
dessertspoonfuls onto a hot greased griddle or heavy iron pan
and cook over medium heat until nicely browned underneath,
turn and cook on the other side. Be sure to cook right through.
Serve hot with lots of butter.

POTATO CAKES (TRADITIONAL)

75 g (3 oz) plain flour   ½ teasp. salt
½ teasp. baking powder   25 g (1 oz) butter
200 g (½ lb) mashed potato   1 tablesp. milk

Sieve the flour, salt and baking powder into a bowl, rub in the
butter until the mixture resembles fine breadcrumbs, then mix
in the mashed potato and a little milk to make a soft dough.

Roll out 1½ cm (½ inch) thick on a floured board, cut into shapes with a small round cutter, brush with beaten egg and bake in a hot oven (215° C gas mark 7) for about 15 to 20 minutes. Serve hot with lashings of butter. Delicious fried in hot fat, too, and served with sausages or rashers of bacon.

Traditional Soda Bread

Irish soda bread is quick and easy to make and for some reason it gains one an instant reputation as a wonderful cook and a devoted mother! It is usually referred to as White or Brown 'Cake' in Ireland and is on sale in some shops; if it looks yellowish this is a sign that too much bread soda has been added. Traditionally it was always made with sour milk or buttermilk, now-a-days we use fresh milk and add cream of tartar instead.

WHITE SODA BREAD (TRADITIONAL)

900 g (2 lb) plain flour
2 teasp. cream of tartar
  (Bextartar)
600 ml (1 pint) milk
1 teasp. salt

1 teasp. bread soda (bicarbonate of soda)

Sieve the flour, soda, cream of tartar and salt into a mixing bowl. Pour the milk into a well in the centre of the mixture, and mix with a knife blade until most of the flour is taken up. Now knead with floured hands, adding more milk if necessary – the dough should be rather soft. Shape the dough into a round flattish cake, about 22 cm (9 inches) across and place on a floured baking tin. Cut a cross on top to allow for rising and bake in a fairly hot oven (205° C gas mark 6) for an hour or more, covering with foil about half way through cooking time so that it does not get too brown.

RAISIN BREAD

The same as White Soda Bread, but add: one tablespoon of

sugar and 170 g (6 oz) raisins to the flour before mixing in the milk.

BROWN SODA BREAD (TRADITIONAL)

560 g (1¼ lb) wholemeal flour	1½ teasp. salt
340 g (¾ lb) plain flour	About 600 ml (1 pint) milk
1½ teasp. bread soda	3 teasp. cream of tartar
(bicarbonate of soda)	(Bextartar)

Sieve the white flour, bread soda, cream of tartar and salt into a bowl, lightly mix in the wholemeal flour by allowing it to sift through your fingers, and then proceed as for White Soda Bread. When the bread is done, it will have a hollow sound if you rap your knuckles against the bottom in the way countless Irish women have tested their 'cakes' for generations! Give the bread time to get quite cold before cutting it, it will crumble badly if cut too soon.

BARM BRACK (TRADITIONAL)

450 g (1 lb) plain flour	90 g (3 oz) sugar
60 g (2 oz) butter	1 egg
110 g (4 oz) sultanas	110 g (4 oz) raisins
60 g (2 oz) mixed peel	300 ml (½ pint) milk
½ teasp. cinnamon	1 teasp. salt
20 g (¾ oz) yeast	

Yeast needs sugar, moisture and a little heat to become active, so the mixing bowl and the ingredients must be lukewarm and the dough must be set to rise in a warmish moist atmosphere. Too much heat will kill the yeast. Mix the yeast with ¾ teaspoon of sugar, ¾ teaspoon flour and one tablespoon of lukewarm water in a warmed bowl, until creamy, then cover and leave in a warm place to rise into bubbles, (about 15 minutes). Place the fruit in a very slow oven to warm slightly and swell a little. Warm the mixing bowl, sift the flour, salt and cinnamon into it, rub in the butter, then add the sugar. Keep in a warm place while you beat the egg and heat the milk until tepid, pour both into the flour mixture with the creamed yeast. Beat well for 10 minutes with a wooden spoon until the dough is pliable and elastic, then add the fruit and beat again. Turn the mixture into a warm oiled tin, cover with a damp cloth and leave in a warm draught free place (possibly the airing cupboard?) for about 1 to 1½ hours, until it has risen to double its size. Bake in a moderately hot oven (205° C gas mark 6) for about 40 minutes, brush the top with beaten egg mixed with a pinch of salt to give a glossy finish, and return to the oven for 5 minutes. When done, it will have a hollow sound if tapped. In Ireland Barm Brack is always baked with the following additions at Hallowe'en: a ring, foretelling marriage within the year, a match stick for a wife-beater, a dried pea for riches, a dried bean for permanent bachelorhood and a tiny scrap of cloth ('the rag') signifying poverty.

CHRISTMAS PUDDING MADE WITH GUINNESS

220 g (½ lb) brown sugar
330 g (¾ lb) sultanas
110 g (¼ lb) glacé cherries
110 g (¼ lb) flour
3 eggs
1 teasp. mixed spice
220 g (½ lb) shredded suet
220 g (½ lb) raisins
110 g (¼ lb) mixed peel
110 g (¼ lb) breadcrumbs
½ teasp. salt
1 teasp. cinnamon
150 ml (¼ pint) Guinness, (or 5 tablesp. milk and 3 tablesp. Irish Whiskey)

Clean the fruit, and leave in a very slow heat to swell. Put the sugar, finely chopped suet, sifted flour, breadcrumbs, salt, mixed spice and cinnamon all in a large bowl and mix by running through the fingers. Add the prepared fruit, mix again, then stir in the beaten eggs and Guinness (or milk and Irish Whiskey). Mix well again then put the mixture into 2 well greased pudding bowls. Cover with two layers of foil, well tied down, and bring a loop of the string across the top to form a handle for lifting. Boil for 4 to 5 hours; when done remove the foil and let the top dry a little, then re-cover and store away. This pudding may be made several weeks ahead, and reboiled for two hours before use. Serve hot with Irish Whiskey Butter, or cream.

IRISH WHISKEY BUTTER

100 g (4 oz) castor sugar
1 tablesp. Irish Whiskey
50 g (2 oz) butter

Cream the butter and sugar in a bowl until fluffy, add whiskey and mix well, keep in a cool place until needed.

To flame the pudding: heat a tablespoon, fill with whiskey set alight with a match, pour over the pudding.

PORTER CAKE (TRADITIONAL)

340 g (12 oz) flour
220 g (8 oz) brown sugar
110 g (4 oz) raisins
60 g (2 oz) mixed peel
150 ml (¼ pint) Guinness
¼ teasp. bread soda (bicarbonate of soda)
110 g (4 oz) butter
220 g (8 oz) sultanas
60 g (2 oz) glace cherries
½ teasp. salt
½ teasp. mixed spice
3 eggs

Clean the fruit and leave to swell in very low heat. Cream the sugar and butter with the hand mixer or a wooden spoon, until light and fluffy, then beat the eggs and mix in. Sift the flour, salt and mixed spice and fold in with a metal spoon, add the prepared fruit and finally the bread soda (bicarbonate of soda) dissolved in the Guinness. Mix well.

Line a well greased 20 cm (8 inch) cake tin with foil inside, and several thicknesses of grease-proof paper around the outside. Put in the mixture, leaving a slight hollow in the centre to allow for rising, and bake for about 2 hours in a very moderate oven (180° C gas mark 4) covering with grease-proof paper after an hour to prevent overbrowning. Test with a warmed skewer thrust into the cake several times – if no crumbs adhere to it, the cake is done. Cool on a wire rack, remove the foil when the cake is cold. Porter Cake is very good on its own, but if you want to ice it, brush the top and sides with warm melted jam to stop crumbs mixing with the frosting as you spread it, then cover with Lemon Frosting.

LEMON FROSTING

30 g (1 oz) butter
1 dessertsp. grated orange rind
12 whole almonds
280 g (10 oz) icing sugar
1 tablesp. lemon juice

Cream the butter, beat in the lemon juice and finely grated orange rind, then add the sifted icing sugar a little at a time, beating well between each addition. Spread over the cake and decorate with split almonds.

Carrageen Moss

Carrageen Moss is a type of seaweed which is gathered from the rocks and dried in the sun. It is good for the health because it contains iodine, but rather insipid unless combined with something which has more flavour.

CARRAGEEN CREAM (TRADITIONAL)

15 g (½ oz) Carrageen Moss   600 ml (1 pint) milk
60 g (2 oz) sugar   Pinch of salt
A few thin strips of lemon rind

Soak the dried Carrageen in cold water for about 20 minutes, drain and boil with the milk, salt and lemon rind for 15 minutes over a low heat, stirring occasionally. This thickens the milk slightly, it will set a bit more when cold. Strain through a sieve, discard the seaweed and return the milk to the saucepan with the sugar. Heat until the sugar is dissolved, pour into a mould and leave to set in a cold place. This can be used instead of custard with stewed fruit; it is pleasant with canned peaches.

CARRAGEEN BANANA CREAM (my recipe)

600 ml (1 pint) Carrageen
   Cream (recipe above)
25 g (1 oz) crystallized ginger   3 bananas
25 g (1 oz) brown sugar   15 g (½ oz) ground
a little whipped cream   almonds
a few whole almonds

Slice the bananas, add with the crystallized ginger cut into small dice, the brown sugar and ground almonds to the luke warm Carrageen Cream. Mix gently, spoon into individual jelly glasses and chill. Serve very cold, decorated with whipped cream and whole almonds.

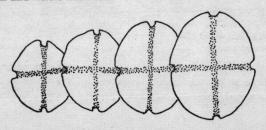

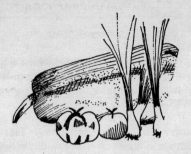

A Variety of Ways with Vegetables

When buying vegetables choose them small, crisp and fresh; try to use as soon as possible after buying them. Green vegetables may be crisped up by soaking in cold water before cooking.

The sauces most commonly used with cooked vegetables are White (Bechamel) Sauce, Hollandaise Sauce and French Dressing, they are included here for easy reference.

WHITE SAUCE, OF COATING CONSISTENCY

25 g (1 oz) butter 25 g (1 oz) flour
250 ml ($\frac{1}{2}$ pint) milk Salt and pepper

Melt the butter in a saucepan, mix in the flour until thickened, add milk by degrees stirring continuously, and boil for about three minutes until smooth and creamy (the hand mixer is useful for the removal of any lumps). A tiny pinch of mace or nutmeg, half a teaspoon mustard, chopped parsley or grated cheese may be added according to recipe, and a tablespoon of cream added at the last moment gives a velvety texture.

HOLLANDAISE SAUCE (economical recipe)

3 tablesp. white vinegar or 2 tablesp. water
   lemon juice
1 large egg or 2 yolks 50 g (2 oz) butter
Salt and pepper

Beat the egg in a small bowl, add the mixed vinegar and water a little at a time, beating briskly. Cut the butter into small cubes, add half to the egg and vinegar mixture, place the bowl in a saucepan of boiling water and cook over very gentle heat (the water in the saucepan should be barely simmering) stirring continuously. When the sauce has thickened a little, add the remaining butter by degrees still beating well. Season with a little salt and pepper, keep warm in a pan of lukewarm water if it has to wait. Make this sauce very slowly as otherwise it may curdle. If it does, all is not lost: pour the curdled sauce gradually into a cold basin containing another eggyolk, beating well, then proceed over hot water as before once the sauce is smooth again.

FRENCH DRESSING

1 tablesp. wine vinegar   3 tablesp. olive oil
Salt and freshly ground black
  pepper

Put all the ingredients into a small jar, screw on the lid and shake briskly for a minute or two. ½ teasp. sugar and chopped herbs may be added.

ARTICHOKES, GLOBE

Allow one or two per person according to size. Wash, and trim the stalks, plunge into boiling water to which is added salt, a nut of butter and a little lemon juice and boil for 20 to 30 minutes according to age. They are done as soon as the leaves come away when pulled gently.

Serve on hot plates with individual pots of melted butter to which is added a little salt, black pepper, and a squeeze of lemon juice. The delicious nut of flesh at the base of each leaf is dipped into the butter then squeezed off between the teeth; the hairy choke is discarded, and then the most succulent part, the heart, is eaten dripping with butter. Good also with Hollandaise sauce; or served cold with a French Dressing.

ARTICHOKES, JERUSALEM

Wash and scrape the artichokes, putting them into cold water with a little vinegar – this will stop them going discoloured. Bring a saucepan of water to the boil, adding salt and half a teaspoon of vinegar to each 600 ml (1 pint), put in the artichokes and boil gently for about 20 minutes until soft. Drain well, serve garnished with pats of butter and chopped parsley or with creamy white sauce.

ASPARAGUS

Scrape the bottom of the stalks lightly, wash in cold water and tie in bundles of 8 to 10, with all their tips in one direction. Put into boiling salted water with a nut of butter and a squeeze of lemon juice, boil gently for about 20 to 30 minutes until tender. Lift out carefully or the tips may fall off, serve with melted butter to which salt and pepper is added, or with Hollandaise sauce (page 103). If served cold, accompany with French Dressing. There is nothing to equal the flavour of fresh asparagus.

BEANS, FRENCH AND RUNNER

Beans should be eaten young and freshly picked, test by bending double, they should snap in two.

Cut off both ends, and a narrow strip down each side to remove the strings which are very tough if left on. Cut the beans into small slices in a slanting direction, or better still in long thin strips from top to bottom. Put into boiling salted water with a little sugar added and cook uncovered for 15 to 25 minutes, according to age.

When tender, drain and serve garnished with small pats of butter. Delicious with very crisply fried rashers crumbled over the top; or mushrooms thinly sliced through the cap and stalk, fried in butter and mixed with the beans. Left over beans may be tossed in French Dressing (page 104) and served cold.

BROAD BEANS

These can be eaten at three stages:

(a) When the beans are very young, cut both ends off the pod and cook whole, until tender, in boiling salted water, serve with onion chopped very finely and fried in butter until golden brown, and spooned over the beans.

(b) When the beans in the pod are about 1½ cm (½ inch) long, shell them and cook uncovered in boiling salted water for about 20 minutes, serve with butter and black pepper; delicious also with leftover chopped ham mixed through them.

(c) Rather old pods containing large beans should not be wasted. Pod the beans, boil for 25 to 35 minutes in boiling salted water until the skins are loose, pinch one end and squeeze the contents out. Heat in melted butter and serve garnished with chopped chives – they have a delicious nutty flavour.

BROCCOLI, PURPLE SPROUTING

Buy carefully, as purple sprouting brocolli becomes very stringy towards the end of its season.

Wash in cold salted water, tie in bundles, all stalks lying in one direction, put into boiling salted water and cook gently for about 15 minutes until the stalks are tender. Drain well and serve with melted butter or Hollandaise sauce (page 103); combines very well with pork, or steak and kidney pie.

BRUSSELS SPROUTS

Choose sprouts that are small, green and firm, the large loose-leaved ones are apt to be soggy when cooked.

Remove only discoloured outer leaves, wash well and make a crisscross cut on the base of each stalk to shorten the cooking times. Put into boiling salted water, and cook for 10 to 12 minutes until just soft but not mushy. Drain well and serve with butter; crisply fried bacon rashers crumbled over make a pleasant contrast. Try Brussels Sprouts with Chestnuts: you need about 12 chestnuts to each ½ kg (1 lb) sprouts. Remove the chestnut skins, boil until tender, and chop finely. Mix with the cooked drained sprouts, pour a little melted butter over, serve hot.

CABBAGE

Cabbage is the most sadly abused vegetable of all, it is often boiled into a colourless, flavourless mush. Choose the crisp firm heads, if it is rather limp freshen up by soaking in cold water for half an hour or so.

Spring Cabbage. Wash in cold water, cut into quarters, put into boiling salted water, and cook for 8 to 10 minutes, until tender. Do not overcook. Drain well, serve with small pats of butter dotted over; good also with a small pinch of mace or chopped chives.

Savoy cabbage is prepared in the same way, but cooked for 10 to 12 minutes; this is also excellent for Coleslaw salad.

Firmly-hearted white cabbage. Remove the discoloured outer leaves, hold under cold running water – in the case of firm tightly packed cabbage this is often all the washing needed. Cut into quarters, discard the hard centre stalk, and shred finely, cutting across the leaves. Plunge into boiling salted water, to which you have added a little sugar, cook for 10 to 12 minutes until tender but slightly crisp to bite. Drain well and serve with a pinch of nutmeg, and melted butter; or a little thick cream, topped with rashers crisply fried, then crumbled over.

Instead of cooking in the ordinary way, as above, the shredded cabbage may be drained after only two minutes of boiling. Then melt a tablespoon of butter or bacon fat in a saucepan, add the cabbage, a pinch of mace, a squeeze of lemon juice, salt and pepper, and cook gently with the lid on over a low heat for about 12 to 15 minutes, stirring occasionally. The cabbage should be slightly crunchy when done, the flavour is excellent.

SWEET–SOUR CABBAGE

1 medium white cabbage	1 tablesp. cooking oil
1 tablesp. honey or sugar	4 tablesp. cider
1 dessertsp. wine vinegar	2 teasp. flour
A pinch of cinnamon	Salt and black pepper

Discard the discoloured outer leaves, cut the cabbage into four, remove the hard stalk, shred the leaves. Heat the cooking oil in a saucepan with the honey or sugar for about two minutes, make sure it does not get overbrowned. Add the cabbage and mix by lifting lightly with a fork until it is coated with oil, then put in the cinnamon, salt and pepper, cider and vinegar. Cook gently over a low heat with the lid on, stirring occasionally. After about 10 minutes, mix the flour with 4 tablespoons of water, pour over the cabbage, and cook covered for another 10 minutes, stirring now and then. The cabbage should be tender but slightly crisp. Very good with roast pork, or fried sausage. White cabbage is also excellent raw in salads (page 119).

CARROTS

Tender young carrots should be gently scraped (try using a nylon potscraper to do this) then cooked whole if small, or cut into quarters lengthways if larger. Cook in a little boiling water, just sufficient to cover, with a nut of butter, a pinch of sugar, salt and pepper until tender, drain off any remaining water (most will have evaporated) and serve with small pats of butter dotted over, and a sprinkling of freshly chopped mint.

Older carrots should be very thinly peeled, then cut into rings, long narrow lengths or short very thin strips like match sticks. Boil until tender in salted water, or better still, well flavoured stock, drain and serve with melted butter, and chopped parsley, chives or mint. They may also be covered with a creamy white sauce (page 103).

CAULIFLOWER AND BROCCOLI

Although in season at different times of the year, these two vegetables are very similar and may be cooked in the same way.

Trim the base of the stalk and make a criss-cross cut to hasten cooking; strip off any discoloured outer leaves but do not remove the fresh green ones. Soak in cold water for about 30 minutes, the head may be divided into about 8 sprigs or left whole. Place, stalk down, in boiling·salted water and cook uncovered for 15 to 20 minutes until the stalk is tender when tested with the point of a knife – the cut sprigs will take a little less time. Lift out very carefully, drain well and serve with melted butter and a little lemon juice, garnish with chopped parsley or chives. Alternatively, breadcrumbs may be browned in butter and sprinkled over or it may be served with white sauce.

CAULIFLOWER, TOMATO AND BACON
(serves 4 to 6)

1 large cauliflower	6 rashers streaky bacon
6 medium tomatoes	1 large onion
25 g (1 oz) butter or	1 tablesp. olive oil
1 tablesp. chopped parsley	½ teasp. sugar
Salt and pepper	50 g (2 oz) grated cheese
600 ml (1 pint) white sauce (page 103)	

Cook the cauliflower for about 12 minutes (it should not be too soft), drain well and keep hot. Pour boiling water over the tomatoes, remove the skins, and cut into slices. Cut the rashers into small strips, chop the onion, and fry together in the oil or butter for about 10 minutes; add the sliced tomatoes, sugar, parsley, and salt and pepper to taste, cover and cook over low heat for another 10 minutes.

Divide the cauliflower, including the stalk, into several large pieces, arrange them in a buttered ovenproof dish, spoon the tomato mixture over, then cover with white sauce. Scatter the grated cheese (preferably Gruyere) over the top, and brown in the oven or under the grill.

This is an economical supper dish; use a 370 g (13 oz) tin of peeled whole tomatoes when fresh ones are dear.

CELERIAC

Useful in winter as a cooked vegetable or in salads, may be used for flavouring instead of celery; it looks like a turnip.

Wash, peel and slice the celeriac, put into cold water with a little vinegar to prevent discolouration. Put into boiling salted water with a little vinegar added, and cook for about 20 to 30 minutes until tender. Drain well, serve with butter and chopped chives or coat with White Sauce (page 103).

CELERY

A delicous winter vegetable which is eaten either raw or cooked, the leaves as well as the stalks may be used for flavouring soups and stews, and may also be chopped and added to turkey or chicken stuffing.

Method: Wash very carefully in cold salty water as it is apt to harbour slugs and earthworms. If eating raw scrape any brown marks off the stalks, put into cold water to crisp, and eat dipped in salt. Braised Celery: Plunge into boiling water for 5 minutes, than place in a casserole with a little chopped bacon, sliced onion and sliced carrot, add stock, cover closely and simmer for $1\frac{1}{2}$ to 2 hours in a very moderate oven (170° C gas mark 3). Also good boiled, and served with white sauce.

CHICORY (OR ENDIVE)

This may be used for salads, or braised in the same manner as celery (recipe above).

LEEKS

Method: Wash very carefully to get rid of the earth which sometimes gets down between the layers, put into boiling salted water and cook without a lid on for about 20 minutes until tender. Serve with melted butter and chopped parsley, or coated with White Sauce.

LEEKS WITH TOMATOES (serves 4 to 6)

6 to 8 medium leeks	4 large tomatoes
2 tablesp. olive oil	Salt and paprika pepper
1 clove garlic (optional)	1 teasp. sugar
1 tablesp. chopped parsley	1 teasp. lemon juice

Trim and wash the leeks, cut into short lengths and wash again under running water. Heat the oil in a heavy frying pan, fry the leeks gently for 10 minutes, stirring to prevent scorching which happens very easily. Add the tomatoes, peeled and chopped (tinned ones if the fresh ones are very dear), sugar, crushed garlic, salt and pepper, and cook rather fast for 5 minutes until much of the juice has evaporated. Add the lemon juice, and serve garnished with chopped parsley – very good with lamb or pork.

MARROWS

Vegetable marrows should be eaten when young and tender, preferably the size of a large pear when they are called cour-gettes.

Large marrows: peel and cut into finger-sized pieces. Melt a little butter in a saucepan, add a small onion very finely chopped (optional), the sliced marrow, some chopped parsley and salt and pepper, cover closely and simmer without any added liquid over a low heat for 10 minutes. Good also with a few peeled chopped tomatoes, and a dessertspoon of sultanas added at the start of cooking time.

Marrows may also be cut in half lengthways and stuffed, then baked in the oven.

Baby marrows (courgettes): wash but do not peel, put whole into boiling salted water for 2 minutes, then pour the water off. Add a good knob of butter, chopped parsley and chives, and salt and pepper; cover closely and simmer for 20 minutes until tender. Cut in half for serving, put a pat of butter on each section and a sprinkling of salt and freshly ground black pepper, eat the seeds as well as the flesh. They may also be cooked in the same way as large marrows.

MUSHROOMS

Mushrooms are very versatile, useful for breakfast and savouries, as a garnish for meat and vegetables, made into soup, cooked as a vegetable or raw in salads. There is no waste in cultivated mushrooms, use caps and stalks and do not peel if fresh. The field mushrooms must be peeled if discoloured and the stalks are usually discarded, but the flavour is magnificent.

To fry; use just enough butter or oil to cover the bottom of the pan, cook for about 4 minutes over gentle heat until just golden, add a little lemon juice, and salt at the last moment as it makes the juices run.

To grill: Pour boiling water over, rinse in cold water, brush with melted butter and grill for about 2 minutes, salt just before serving on hot buttered toast.

ONIONS

Obtainable all the year round, onions are used more than any other vegetable for adding savoury flavour to a great number of dishes.

Onions may be baked with a roast in the oven: trim but do not peel one large onion per person, put on a baking sheet and bake in a moderately hot oven (205° C gas mark 6) for 1½ to 2 hours, cover with greaseproof paper if getting too brown. Serve each with a good knob of butter, salt and freshly ground black pepper.

To boil onions, peel medium sized onions, put into a large saucepan of boiling salted water and cook until tender but not mushy, the time varies according to size and variety, from 1 to 1½ hours. Serve with melted butter, or White Sauce (page 103) to which grated cheese may be added if liked.

To fry onions remove the brown skin, cut into rings or dice, fry gently in oil, dripping or butter until golden brown, stirring occasionally to prevent scorching. Season to taste – the classic partner to grilled steak.

PARSNIPS

Wash, scrape carefully to remove all discoloured parts, leave whole if small, cut into quarters if large. Put into boiling salted water, and cook for about 40 minutes, or more if old; they should be soft but firm. Serve with butter and garnish with chopped chives or parsley; they may also be coated with White Sauce (page 103). Alternatively, mash finely or put through the blender, and serve mixed with a little cream and a pinch of mace.

PEAS

As peas lose their fresh sweet flavour very soon after being picked, choose very carefully – the pods should be firm, green and shiny, the peas inside small; rough whitish pods indicate hard and bitter peas within.

Shell the peas, put into boiling salted water with ¼ teaspoon of sugar added for each cup of water. Drop in a sprig of fresh mint and cook for 10 to 15 minutes, drain and serve dotted with small pats of butter.

Peas with young carrots make a delectable and colourful combination in Spring. Scrape small young carrots, cut into dice and put with a knob of butter into just enough boiling salted water to cover. Cook without a lid for 10 minutes, add the tiny shelled peas and boil uncovered again for 10 to 15 minutes, adding a little more water if necessary. Drain and serve dotted with small pats of butter and garnished with freshly chopped mint.

POTATOES

Most of the vitamin content of potatoes lies just below the skin, so it is a good idea to cook them in their jackets.

To bake potatoes, scrub large old or new potatoes, prick with a fork and bake in their jackets in a moderate oven (195° C gas mark 5) for 1 to 1½ hours. Serve with plenty of butter, salt and freshly ground black pepper. These may also be stuffed; cut the tops off, spoon out the contents, mix with butter, seasoning and a little chopped ham or grated cheese, put the mixture back into the potato jackets and reheat before serving.

New Potatoes are usually washed and scraped (try using a nylon potscraper), boil in salted water with a sprig of mint. Cook until just tender, drain, and put a knob of butter in the saucepan to melt, shake the pan until all the potatoes are coated. Serve garnished with freshly chopped mint or parsley – the flavour is sweet and nutty. New potatoes also make an excellent potato salad (page 119).

Old Potatoes for steaming must be washed well but not peeled. Put into cold salted water and bring to the boil with the lid on. Cook for about 15 minutes, then drain the water off, cover with a folded tea towel and the lid, steam slowly over low heat until tender when tested with a skewer. This way of finishing ensures they will be dry and floury, instead of being cooked down to a mush.

Left Over Boiled Potatoes. Fry a little onion in butter until golden, add the peeled and sliced potatoes, salt and pepper and cook until hot right through. A little chopped ham or bacon adds flavour.

Fluffy Mashed Potatoes. Peel thinly, put into cold salted water and bring to the boil, cook with the lid on until tender (about 25 minutes). Drain well, return to heat for a few minutes to dry out, then add hot milk at the rate of 1 cup to 6 medium sized potatoes, salt and a lump of butter, and beat until light and fluffy – the hand mixer gives a lovely smooth finish. Sprinkle a little Cayenne or Paprika pepper over for colour contrast.

Left Over Mashed Potato. Put into a shallow greased oven-proof dish, brush with beaten egg and brown in the oven. Alternatively, mix 450 g (1 lb) mashed potato with one beaten egg and a little chopped onion and parsley, form into round flat cakes, coat with egg and bread crumbs and fry in hot fat until crisp and golden.

For Potato Chips, peel the potatoes, cut into thick slices and then into finger-sized chips, soak in cold water for a few

minutes, remove and dry thoroughly. Fry in very deep hot fat
or oil – when a small cube of bread is dropped in it should
form little bubbles and rise to the surface, this shows the fat is
hot enough. If the fat is not really hot, the chips will be greasy
and broken. Fry until light golden and crisp outside and floury
inside, drain on kitchen paper, sprinkle salt over and serve
immediately.

SPINACH

Spinach cooks down in the most amazing way, allow about
1 kg (2½ lb) for 4 people. Wash well in cold water, tear out the
white centre stalks, put the green leaves into a large saucepan
containing boiling salted water, and cook without a lid for 10
to 12 minutes. Drain well, pressing out as much water as
possible, chop very finely with a sharp knife or put through
the blender with cream and lemon juice added to make it
sufficiently liquid. Reheat in a little melted butter, adding a
squeeze of lemon juice and 4 tablespoons of cream if not added
when blending.

SWEDE TURNIPS

Cut into large chunks and cook and serve as for parsnips
(page 113). Good also boiled with bacon.

TOMATOES

Tomatoes, like mushrooms and onions are used in many
savoury dishes. Choose those which are shiny, firm and well
coloured, avoid imported ones with a small black spot near
the stalk as they go bad very quickly. Unevenly shaped tomatoes often have excellent flavour, as do the tiny ones which are
often sold very cheaply when home grown tomatoes are in
season.
When peeling tomatoes leave for 20 seconds in a bowl of

boiling water then pour cold water over – the skin will strip off easily.

Grilled Tomatoes. Cut in half, brush with a little oil, sprinkle with salt and pepper and grill for 4 to 5 minutes.

Baked Tomatoes. Cut the large ones in half, season with salt and pepper, top with breadcrumbs and a pat of butter, and bake in a moderate oven (195° C gas mark 5) for about 15 minutes, garnish with chopped parsley or chives. Small tomatoes may be baked whole.

WHITE TURNIPS

Cook and serve in the same manner as parsnips (page 113), but allow only about 20 minutes boiling for small young turnips.

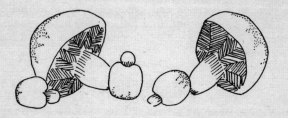

Salads and Herbs

Salads

Use only young, crisp and freshly gathered ingredients for
salads, and be sure that all the moisture is removed after
washing. Lettuce usually forms the basis of most salads, but
tender Spring greens, fresh young spinach, nasturtium leaves
or water cress may be used as salad greens, especially when
lettuce is expensive.

MIXED SALAD

Using salad greens as a base, choose from the following to
make individual combinations of flavour and colour: tomatoes,
hard boiled eggs, (halved bantam's eggs are particularly
appealing), black olives, white turnip, small green peas, young
carrots either sliced or grated, celery, spring onions, cucumber,
radishes, sliced oranges, pineapple pieces, slices of unpeeled
red apples (sprinkled with lemon juice to stop browning), thinly
sliced green or red peppers (discard the seeds), endive, flowerettes of cauliflower, and raw sliced mushrooms soaked in oil
and lemon juice.

Cooked vegetables such as potatoes sliced or cubed, carrots,
peas, asparagus, green beans, artichoke hearts and beetroot
(well dried or the red juice will discolour the rest of the salad)
can all be used.

Garnish with sliced stuffed olives, capers, chopped herbs,

sieved hardboiled egg yolk, sprigs of parsley or chopped
walnuts or almonds.

Arrange the chosen ingredients either in a salad bowl or on a
large flat dish and hand separately creamy yellow home-made
Mayonnaise (page 31) or pep up shop bought Mayonnaise
like this; to each ½ cup of Mayonnaise add 3 tablespoons of
whipped cream, 2 teaspoons of lemon juice and ½ a teaspoon
of sugar, mix well.

LOW CALORIE SALAD DRESSING

1 carton plain yogurt	1 egg yolk
¼ teasp. salt	A pinch Cayenne pepper
¼ teasp. mustard	2 teasp. lemon juice
¼ clove crushed garlic (optional)	½ teasp. sugar

Blend all the ingredients except the yogurt together in a small
bowl until creamy, add the yogurt a little at a time, mixing
well, chill before serving.

SOME SUGGESTIONS FOR SALADS

(1) Diced cooked beetroot, diced apple and chopped celery,
topped with a few chopped nuts.

(2) Sliced cooked beetroot and sliced raw onion in vinegar.

(3) Sliced cucumber, sliced orange, sliced hard boiled eggs,
and cauliflower flowerettes arranged on a bed of lettuce,
garnished with chopped chives – the combination of white,
yellow and crisp green looks inviting.

(4) Cooked diced carrots and cooked peas mixed with
Mayonnaise, served on a bed of shredded raw cabbage.

(5) Cut thin slices of cucumber, sprinkle with salt and leave
for an hour to drain off some of the juice, serve in a bowl with
plain yogurt poured over. Pickled cucumber also combines
well with yogurt.

(6) Quartered tomatoes, quartered hard boiled eggs, thinly
sliced green pepper (4 rings for each person, discard the pips),
small radishes and pineapple pieces. Each ingredient is
arranged in a separate group on a bed of lettuce; garnish with
black grapes halved and pipped.

GREEN SALAD

Choose very crisp hearts of lettuce, separate the leaves and wash well in cold water, drain and shake dry in a salad basket, or a clean dry tea towel. Rub the salad bowl with a cut clove of garlic to give a delicate tang, tear the lettuce leaves into two or three pieces (never use a knife to cut lettuce) and arrange in the bowl garnished with chopped parsley or chives.

Mix half a teaspoon of sugar into French Dressing (page 104) and sprinkle just enough over to coat the lettuce, mixing gently to see that all the leaves are covered. As the lettuce wilts very soon after this dressing is added, serve at once. Small spring onions, sliced cucumber or watercress may be included.

COLESLAW (serves 4 to 6)

1 small firm white cabbage	2 tablesp. chopped celery
3 tablesp. lemon juice	2 tablesp. sultanas
1 tablesp. finely chopped onion (opt.)	2 teasp. sugar
3 tablesp. olive oil	1 teasp. salt

Cut the cabbage into quarters, discard the hard stalk and cut into very fine shreds, leave to crisp in cold water for half an hour. Wash the sultanas, dry and leave to soak in lemon juice. Drain and dry the cabbage carefully, mix with the sultanas (keep the lemon juice) chopped celery and finely chopped onion. Put the reserved lemon juice, sugar, olive oil, and salt into a small jar, screw on the lid and shake well for a minute or two, pour it over the cabbage mixture lifting lightly with a fork so that all is coated. Serve at once.

POTATO SALAD (serves 6)

1 kg (2 lb) boiled potatoes	1 tablesp. chopped onion
½ a cup French Dressing	1 cup Mayonnaise
Chopped chives	

Cut the hot potatoes into cubes or thin slices, mix with very finely chopped onion and pour the French Dressing over while the potato is still warm, leave to cool. Arrange in a flattish dish, pour the Mayonnaise over and garnish with chopped chives.

Herbs

Fresh herbs add enormously to the flavour, aroma and individual character of savoury dishes. The following are perennials, and many of them are easily grown from seed or cuttings: bay, chives, fennel, mint, rosemary, rue, sage, sweet marjorum, tarragon and thyme. Annual herbs grown from seed are: balm, basil, borage, chervil, coriander, dill and parsley. Many herbs may be grown in pots on a sunny window-sill, but should be kept well pinched back to prevent 'legginess'. Failing a home-grown supply the dried herbs which are sold in cannisters keep their flavour for a long time if kept tightly closed.

A bouquet garni consists of a *bayleaf*, 3 sprigs of *parsley* and a spring of *thyme* tied in a small bunch and added to soups, stews and sauces. The chopped leaves of *balm, basil, coriander, chervil, fennel, marjorum, savory* or *tarragon* add flavour to soups, stews, sauces, stuffing and savoury dishes.

Some herbs have an affinity with certain flavours:

(1) Try a thick layer of chopped *basil*, or a little chopped *tarragon* over sliced tomatoes.

(2) *Chives* are most versatile; snip them with scissors and scatter over new potatoes, carrots, cream soups or salads; combine them with cream cheese, scrambled eggs, mashed potatoes or sandwich fillings.

(3) *Dill* or *fennel* are excellent with stewed mutton and fish, add the chopped leaves to the sauce; add to French dressing; or snip them over French beans or cucumber. The feathery leaves make a most attractive garnish.

(4) *Garlic* has a very strong smell and flavour and should be used cautiously in soups, stews, sauces and savoury dishes – one clove is usually enough for 3 or 4 helpings. Before using, crush each clove with the blade of a knife against the edge of a plate, having added a little salt, or use a garlic press. Small slivers of garlic may be inserted into a joint of lamb or mutton before roasting, or a cut clove of garlic rubbed around a salad bowl imparts a delicious and delicate tang.

(5) Include a sprig of *rosemary* in the parcel with a leg of mutton or lamb for roasting, or chop the leaves very finely and add to lamb stew.

(6) *Sage* and *thyme* are strongly flavoured and should be rather sparingly used in stuffing.

(7) Although not a herb this is such a delicious flavouring that I include it here: when cooking gooseberries for a pudding or for jam dip a few flowerheads of the *elderberry* into the boiling fruit just before the end of cooking time – the gooseberries will taste like muscatel grapes.

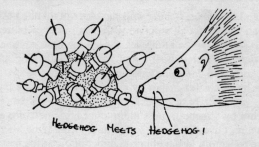

HEDGEHOG MEETS HEDGEHOG!

There's Always Room at Our House

It is fun to entertain one's friends, to invite them in to a party, a meal or just morning coffee and a gossip. Whether you are having a drinks party, a fork supper or a child's birthday tea, the secret is to plan ahead. Choose the menu carefully so that much of it can be prepared in advance; take endless pains over every detail, then relax and enjoy the company; and never apologize for any small short-comings!

The Drinks Party

Plan the 'eats' first, allowing about nine or ten savouries for each person. Make one or two mixes of Rough Puff Pastry three or four days ahead (or buy the ready made kind) as it forms the basis of a variety of savouries which are quick and easy to prepare.

ROUGH PUFF PASTRY

220 g (8 oz) plain flour	90 g (3 oz) lard
90 g (3 oz) butter or margarine	1 teasp. lemon juice
7 to 8 tablesp. cold water	¼ teasp. salt

Sift the flour and the salt into a mixing bowl, cut the butter or margarine, and the lard into cubes the size of walnuts, mix these through the flour without rubbing in. Add the lemon juice and the water, stirring with the blade of a knife until you have an elastic dough studded with small nuts of butter and lard, it should not be at all wet. Knead the pastry into a ball, turn onto a floured board and roll out with long strokes backwards and forwards until it is an oblong shape about 30 cm by 15 cm (12 inches by 6 inches). Fold the pastry into three, you now have a thick piece about 10 cm by 15 cm (4 inches by 6 inches), press along the edges and twice across the centre. Give the pastry half a turn to the right, so that it will be rolled out in the opposite direction from the first time, and roll out again, it will form a long narrow strip. Fold this in three and repeat the pressing down, half turn to the right and roll again, and then do the whole operation again (4 rollings) ending with folding into three, cover it and leave in a cool place for at least an hour. This pastry will keep for four days if wrapped in greaseproof paper, then put into a plastic bag and kept in the refrigerator.

TINY SAUSAGE ROLLS

To make about 30 to 35 small sausage rolls you need: half the quantity of Rough Puff Pastry made as above, 220 g (½ lb) of sausages, and a beaten egg for brushing.

Slit the sausage skins and remove the filling, form the meat into long rolls thinner than a sausage. Roll the pastry out using long smooth strokes, until it is an oblong just thicker than a match stick, cut into strips 5 cm (2 inches) wide, brush lightly with beaten egg and lay the roll of sausage meat along one of the long edges. Fold the pastry strip over the roll of sausage meat, press the cut edges together, slightly overlapping, and cut into short lengths of about 2½ cm (1 inch). Brush the top with beaten egg, cut a small slit in the top of each and bake in a hot oven (220° C gas mark 7) for about 12 minutes until golden brown. These may be eaten fresh from the oven, or cooled and kept in a tin for a day and reheated before serving – it is not safe to keep them longer, nor to reheat more than once.

SMALL PASTRY CASES

Roll out some Rough Puff Pastry very evenly until it is about ½ cm (⅛ inch) thick, cut into rounds with a cutter 2½ cm (1 inch) in diameter, then cut the centre out of half these rounds, using a thimble. Turn all the rounds over, brush the whole ones with beaten egg, then cover each with a round with a hole in the centre, press down lightly; cover with greaseproof paper and leave in a cool place for 30 minutes – this 'rest' will stop the pastry shrinking out of shape as it cooks. Grease a baking sheet lightly, sprinkle with a few drops of water, and place the pastry cases in position. Brush the tops with a little beaten egg, making sure that none runs down the sides, and bake in a very hot oven (230° C gas mark 8) for about 10 minutes, until golden brown and well risen.

The cases, called bouchées, may be made in advance, cooled and kept in a tin for a few days. Fill with a savoury filling (see below) and heat just before serving.

SAVOURY FILLINGS

25 g (1 oz) butter	25 g (1 oz) flour
250 ml (½ pint) milk	¼ teasp. salt

Melt the butter in a saucepan, stir in the flour and salt and cook over low heat until thickened, add the milk by degrees stirring constantly and boil for about 3 minutes until smooth and creamy. One teaspoon of very finely chopped onion, chives or parsley, or a crushed clove of garlic may be added for additional flavour. Then mix into the sauce one of the following: minced chicken, turkey, duck or ham; chopped prawns, shrimps, crab or lobster; chopped mushrooms and a few chopped rashers of streaky bacon fried in butter; mashed salmon or sardines; then add Cayenne or Paprika pepper to taste. Put a little filling into each pastry case, heat and serve.

QUICK CHEESE PUFFS

Roll out a little Rough Puff Pastry (trimmings will do) until as thick as a match stick, cut out rounds with a small pastry

cutter, about 2½ cm (1 inch) in diameter, prick the tops lightly
with a fork and leave covered in a cool place for 30 minutes.
Brush the tops with beaten egg, place ½ a teaspoon of grated
Parmesan cheese on each, and bake in a hot oven (230° C gas
mark 8) for about 7 minutes, watch carefully as they brown
suddenly.

TINY SCONES

This mixture gives about 25 to 30 small scones which are halved
and topped with a savoury mixture, giving about 50 to 60
savouries.

220 g (½ lb) self raising flour
60 g (2 oz) butter or cooking fat   ½ teasp. salt
8 tablesp. milk

Sift the salt, flour and baking powder into a mixing bowl, cut
the butter or fat into small pieces and rub into the flour. Pour
in the milk and mix to a light smooth dough, cover and leave
to stand for a few minutes before rolling out ½ cm (¼ inch)
thick. Cut into small rounds about 2½ cm (1 inch) across, lay
on a lightly greased baking sheet, cover and leave in a cool
place for about 20 minutes then bake in a hot oven (220° C gas
mark 7) for about 15 minutes. These scones may be cooled and
kept in an airtight tin for 2 or 3 days.

Cut the scones in half, butter, then spread with cream cheese
mixed with chopped chives, grated Cheddar cheese mixed with
chutney, cold garlic flavoured scrambled egg, Potted Salmon
(page 58) or Liver Sausage Pate (page 57). Alternatively the
scones may be topped with any of the savoury fillings (page 125)
and heated in the oven for a few minutes before serving.

COCKTAIL SAVOURIES

Use small rounds or squares of fried bread, or toast, or small
crisp biscuits as a base for a colourful and appetizing combination chosen from the following: sliced hard boiled egg, small
pieces of chicken, turkey or ham, salmon, prawns, sliced
tomatoes, cheese, sardines or anchovies. The biscuits or toast

may be spread with fish paste, liver sausage or cream cheese first; the savouries are garnished with stuffed olives, capers, sliced gerkins, parsley, chopped chives or a spot of Mayonnaise.

Fingers of thinly cut brown bread, buttered, and topped with a slice of smoked salmon, a few drops of lemon juice and a leaf of parsley are delicious.

But the choice is limitless, and they are fun to make. If one makes a dozen or two of each kind it is much quicker; prepare them as near party time as possible as they go soggy if kept too long.

CREAMY CHEESE DIP

Beat 90 g (3 oz) cream cheese, 1 teaspoon finely chopped onion, a crushed clove of garlic, ½ teaspoon of salt, a pinch of Cayenne pepper and 3 tablespoons of cream together until smooth and thick, turn into a small dish. Hand around with short lengths of celery, thin crisp fingers of fried bread, or small cheese biscuits which are dipped into the dish before eating.

Tomato Dip and Curry Dip are delicious served hot with small cocktail sausages on sticks for dipping.

SIMPLE SAVOURIES

Stuff dates or large juicy raw prunes with cream cheese after removing the stone.

Hand round potato crisps, salted peanuts or cashew nuts; or white pickled onions, olives or small pieces of cheese on sticks.

A Savoury Hedgehog is rather fun. Put a small cube of cheese, a small piece of tinned pineapple and a white pickled onion one above the other on a cocktail stick and push the other end into half an orange lying on its cut side on a plate – continue until the orange is covered with these 'spines'.

What to Drink?

The choice of drinks is wide – anything from champagne, to sherry, cocktails, white or red wine, beer, mulled wine, 'Cup' or a selection including gin, whiskey, vodka and brandy. If anyone aks for a small drink, give him or her just that. Have a few soft drinks for those who prefer them: pineapple juice, Cidona or tomato juice which can be pepped up with added salt and black pepper, lemon juice, a dash of Worcester sauce and chopped mint; have ice cubes at hand to add at the last moment.

Mulled Wine: good for a winter party, the following quantities serve 6 to 8 people (one wine glass each).

One bottle of red wine such as Claret or Burgundy, the peel of an orange, half a lemon, a piece each of cinnamon and root ginger, two cloves, a pinch of mace, 100 g (4 oz) sugar.

Boil the chopped orange peel, thinly sliced lemon, cinnamon, root ginger, cloves, mace and sugar in 300 ml ($\frac{1}{2}$ pint) water for five minutes, stirring constantly until the sugar melts. Add the red wine, stir and heat until nearly boiling, strain and serve hot.

White Wine Cup: serves 8 to 10 (one wine glass each).

One bottle of Hock or other white wine, and an equal quantity of soda water or lemonade (or a mixture of both), a few leaves of mint, thinly sliced lemon and ice. Add 1 wine glass brandy if liked.

Chill the wine and soda water or lemonade, mix together just before serving, pour into glasses with ice cubes, and garnish each with a slice of lemon and a mint leaf.

Red Wine Cup: substitute the red wine for the white and proceed as for the White Wine Cup, but garnish with thinly sliced orange, the faintest taste of grated nutmeg and ice cubes.

A Beer Party

If the drinks at the party are to be beer and stout (and of course a few soft drinks), provide rather substantial 'eats' such as hot dogs and open sandwiches, made like this: butter slices of several varieties of bread – rye, Vienna, brown soda bread and Crisp bread, and top with rather hearty helpings of a combination of savouries chosen from the following: lettuce, tomato, meat, ham, salmon, shellfish, raw kipper, sardines, grated cheese, cold scrambled eggs, olives and flaked haddock.

Buffet or Fork Supper

To cater for more than six or eight people to a meal a fork supper is a good idea. The menu should be planned so that all the food is manageable with a plate in one hand and a fork in the other.

Welcome your guests with a drink (not forgetting soft drinks for those who prefer them) and salted nuts and crisps. When the party is going well, it is time to eat – the food should all be arranged ready for serving with plates and cutlery to hand. Have two people to dish up the food, the children are useful as waiters, offering second helpings and collecting used plates.

If a little extra is needed with the main course offer home-made brown soda bread sliced and buttered lavishly, or Garlic bread: to butter three Vienna loaves, melt 180 g (6 oz) butter until just liquid with two cloves of crushed garlic and one teaspoon of salt. Slice the Vienna loaves without quite cutting through the bottom crust, brush both sides of each slice and the outside of the loaves with the melted butter, then wrap in tinfoil – this can be done in the morning. Heat when wanted in a moderately hot oven (205° C gas mark 6) for about 15 minutes, serve hot, cutting through the lower crust before handing round.

Cheese and biscuits may be served as a final course: a selection of the many Irish made cheeses such as Gouda, Edam, Cheshire, Cheddar, Blue, Gruyere, Brie and Camembert may be cut into cubes and offered on a tray with small crisp biscuits, previously buttered (this cuts out the necessity for individual cheese plates and knives).

Fork Supper for 20

Menu: Pork Steak with Mushrooms and Cream Sauce
Yellow Rice   Tomato Salad
Fresh Fruit Salad, Boudoir Biscuits and Cream – or –
Meringue Delicious (my own recipe)
Cheese and Biscuits (optional)

PORK STEAKS WITH MUSHROOM AND
CREAM SAUCE

8 pork steaks
900 ml (1½ pints) stock or water
3 tablesp. cooking oil
6 tablesp. sherry (optional)
300 ml (½ pint) cream
½ kg (1lb) mushrooms
Sprigs of parsley for garnish

3 large onions
2 tablesp. flour
3 dessertsp. Paprika pepper
100 g (4 oz) butter
6 tablesp. sultanas
Salt

Reserve half the butter to fry the mushrooms. Heat the remaining butter with the oil in a heavy saucepan, cut the pork steaks across the grain into round bite sized pieces, fry quickly on both sides, remove and keep hot. Fry the chopped onion until golden, return the pork to the saucepan with the sultanas, sprinkle with Paprika and flour, stir, add the stock and sherry if using, bring to the boil. Cover closely with foil or greaseproof paper as well as the lid and simmer over low heat for about an hour, taste for seasoning. If you are preparing this a day in advance, stop here and keep in a cool place until wanted.

Just before the party, reheat the stew over gentle heat, dish into two large casseroles, stir half the cream into each dish and keep hot. Slice the mushrooms through caps and stalks, fry in the reserved butter and scatter over the top of the stew, garnish with the sprigs of parsley, and serve with appetizing yellow rice to mop up the rich cream gravy.

Yellow Rice: for 20 people, boil 1 kg (2 lb) Patna rice in rapidly boiling salted water, to which you have added ½ a teaspoon turmeric, for 12 to 14 minutes until soft to bite but not mushy. Drain through a sieve, hold under the hot tap to separate the grains and dry in a very moderate oven (170° C gas mark 3) for 15 minutes before serving. The rice may be boiled the day before (cook half at a time if you haven't a large enough saucepan) and reheated in a flattish dish covered with buttered paper in a slow oven (155° C gas mark 2) for about 30 minutes before serving. Garnish with chopped parsley.

TOMATO SALAD (serves 20)

750 g (1½ lb) tomatoes
1 tablesp. chopped basil or chives
½ teasp. salt and black pepper
A few drops of chili sauce (optional)

4 medium onions
2 lemons

4 tablesp. olive oil
½ teasp. castor sugar

Put the tomatoes first into boiling water, then into cold water, strip off the skin and slice very thinly into a shallow dish. Sprinkle with a little salt and black pepper, grate the rind of one of the lemons over and cover with a layer of finely chopped onion. Mix together the lemon juice, the oil, sugar, a little salt and black pepper and a few drops of chili sauce if using, and pour over the salad; garnish with chopped basil or chives, leave in a cool place for the flavours to blend.

FRUIT SALAD FOR 20

8 oranges
5 tablesp. sultanas
1 ripe melon
250 g (½ lb) sugar (or more to taste)
300 ml (½ pint) syrup

8 bananas
Juice of 2 lemons
250 g (½ lb) grapes
Minature bottle Cointreau (optional)

The syrup is made as follows: boil 220 g (½ lb) sugar with 300 ml (½ pint) water, or half water and half cider, until the sugar is dissolved, leave to cool.

Put the washed sultanas to soak in the lemon juice, peel the oranges, removing all pith, slice thinly. Cut the melon into cubes or scoop out 'balls' with a teaspoon, peel and pip the grapes. Mix the prepared fruit and lemon juice in a glass bowl with the sugar, then pour in the cold syrup and leave in a cool place (preferably the refrigerator) for a few hours. At the last moment add the sliced bananas (they go brown if put in too soon), and pour in the Cointreau. Serve with whipped cream and Boudoir biscuits.

Other combinations of fruit may be used; Fresh strawberries with sliced oranges and sugar are delicious.

MERINGUE DELICIOUS FOR 20

1 large tin peaches	8 bananas
6 tablesp. sugar	900 ml (1½ pint) whipped cream

For Meringues: (make 2 mixes)

3 egg whites	½ teasp. salt
Small pinch bicarbonate of soda (bread soda)	170 g (6 oz) castor sugar

These ingredients will fill two large bowls. The small meringues may be made a few days in advance and kept in an air-tight tin.

To make meringues; whisk the egg whites with the salt and bread soda until stiff, but not dry. Sift in a quarter of sugar and whisk again until the mixture forms peaks, fold in the rest of the sugar. Brush greaseproof paper on a baking sheet lightly with oil, place small meringues on it, using a forcing bag, or two wet teaspoons for shaping. Dry in a very slow oven (130° C gas mark ½) for an hour or two, peel off the paper and put the meringues into a warm place (the airing cupboard?) to crisp.

Just before serving, have all the ingredients to hand, and combine them like this: using two bowls, arrange layers of meringues (use the broken ones if any) peach cut into small pieces and the juice, whipped cream, sliced banana sprinkled with sugar, whipped cream, and then top with tiny meringues placed close together, eat while the meringues are still crisp. This is a delectable mixture of flavours.

OTHER GOOD DISHES FOR A FORK SUPPER ARE:

(1) Steak Stewed with Guinness (page 90)
(2) Hungarian Beef Stew (page 39)
(3) Dublin Bay Prawns with Yellow Rice (page 96)
(4) Salmon Mayonaise (page 30)

FORK SUPPER FOR 20 TEENAGERS

Menu: Sausages, Grilled Tomatoes, Fried Onions, Fluffy Mashed Potato, Garlic Bread, Demon's Food Chocolate Cake and Vanilla Ice cream

SUGGESTED QUANTITIES FOR MAIN COURSE FOR 20

About 2½ kg (6 lb) sausages
About 4½ kg (10 lb) potatoes
Dripping or oil for frying
Salt and freshly ground black pepper

8 large Spanish onions
20 medium tomatoes
1¼ l (2 pints) milk
110 g (4 oz) butter

Boil the peeled potatoes until soft, mash with about 1¼ l (2 pints) hot milk, butter, salt and black pepper until very light and fluffy (use the hand mixer if you have one), add more hot milk if necessary.

Prick and fry the sausages, slice and fry the onions until golden and serve the halved tomatoes either raw or grilled.

DEMON'S FOOD CHOCOLATE CAKE: MAKE 2 OR 3 FOR 20 PEOPLE

220 g (8 oz) plain flour
1 level teasp. bicarbonate of soda (bread soda)
1 tablesp. white vinegar
110 g (4 oz) butter or margarine
1 teasp. vanilla essence

220 g (8 oz) castor sugar
60 g (2 oz) cocoa
300 ml (½ pint) milk
½ teasp. salt
2 eggs

For the icing:

45 g (1½ oz) butter	1 egg yolk
450 g (1 lb) icing sugar	60 g (2 oz) cocoa
4 tablesp. cream or top milk	½ teasp. vanilla essence

Sift the dry ingredients, flour, sugar, soda, cocoa and salt into a bowl. Mix the vinegar with the milk and vanilla essence, beat the eggs into this mixture, add to the dry ingredients beating well, then beat in the butter or margarine which has been previously melted and cooled (the consistency will be like batter). Line a round cake tin 25 cm (10 ins) in diameter with a loose base and pour in the mixture, bake in a very moderate oven (180° C gas mark 4) for about 50 minutes, covering carefully to prevent over-browning after 20 minutes. Turn out on a wire rack to cool.

For the icing: Cream the egg yolk and the butter, add the sieved icing sugar and cocoa a little at a time alternately with the cream, and add the vanilla essence, beating between each addition, until the icing is light and fluffy.

Split the cake in half, sandwich together with a layer of icing, and spread the remainder over the top and sides of the cake, reserve a little for decoration with an icing syringe.

This cake is beautifully moist, and may be made and iced 2 or 3 days ahead. Slice and serve with icecream – you will need about 4 blocks for 20 people.

INEXPENSIVE FORKSUPPER FOR 20

Menu: Minced Beef with Tomato and Baked Beans (p 64, make 3-4 times the amount)

Home-made Brown Soda Bread sliced and buttered.

Apple Crumble or Rhubarb Crumble (which ever is in season) and Hot Frothy Custard – or Banana Queen of Puddings.

APPLE CRUMBLE (MAKE 3 FOR 20)

1 kg (2 lb) cooking apples	170 g (6 oz) sugar
150 ml (¼ pint) water	¼ teasp. cinnamon
For Crumble:	
110 g (4 oz) sugar	170 g (6 oz) sugar
90 g (3 oz) margarine	

Peel and slice the apples, cook gently until soft in the water, with the 170 g (6 oz) sugar and the cinnamon, put into an ovenproof dish. Sift the flour into a bowl, rub the margarine in until it looks like fine breadcrumbs, lightly mix in the sugar and sprinkle a thick layer of this mixture on top of the fruit. Place the dish in a baking tin containing about 2½ cm (1 inch) of water (this will stop the juice bubbling up through the crumble) and bake in a moderate oven (195° C gas mark 5) for about 40 minutes.

Rhubarb may be substituted for the apple, it will need more sugar.

HOT FROTHY CUSTARD FOR 20

1¼ l (2 pints) milk	2 egg whites
3 rounded dessertsp. custard powder	220 g (½ lb) sugar
2 tablesp. cooking sherry (optional)	

Mix the custard powder to a thin paste with 3 dessertspoons of the milk, bring the rest of the milk to the boil with the sugar. When it rises in the saucepan, pour into the custard mixture in the bowl and stir briskly until it thickens. Allow to cool slightly, stir in the sherry and fold in the stiffly beaten egg whites.

Rhubarb or Apple Crumble and Frothy Custard may also be served cold.

BANANA QUEEN OF PUDDINGS
(MAKE 2 OR 3)

100 g (4 oz) fresh breadcrumbs	2 eggs, separated
25 g (1 oz) margarine or butter	4 tablesp. brown sugar
½ teasp. vanilla essence	¼ teasp. salt
600 ml (1 pint) milk	4 tablesp. jam
3 bananas	2 tablesp. castor sugar

Heat the margarine or butter with the brown sugar until the sugar is dissolved, stir in the milk, salt and vanilla essence, heat until nearly boiling and pour over the breadcrumbs, then allow to cool. Stir in the beaten egg yolks, pour into a large flattish greased pie dish and bake in a moderate oven (195° C gas mark 5) for about 30 minutes until set.

Heat the jam a little and spoon over the pudding; slice the bananas in a layer over the top. Beat the egg whites until stiff, fold in the castor sugar and beat again until the meringue forms peaks, spread over the top and bake in a very slow oven (145° C gas mark 1) for about 30 minutes until golden – serve hot or cold with foamy custard if liked.

Other inexpensive main dishes for a Fork Supper are:
(1) Macaroni Cheese (page 62)
(2) Spaghetti with Hasty Tomato Sauce (page 62)
(3) Spaghetti with Minced Beef (page 63)
(4) Haddock Kedgeree (page 27)
 Inexpensive puddings:

(1) PANCAKES STUFFED WITH SPICY APPLE
(serves 8)

For pancakes:
170 g (6 oz) plain flour
300 ml (½ pint) milk, mixed with 2 tablesp. water

½ teasp. salt
2 eggs
25 to 50 g (1 to 2 oz) lard for frying

For Filling:
450 ml (¾ pint) thick sweetened apple purée
3 tablesp. sultanas soaked in a little sherry

½ teasp. ground cinnamon
2 tablesp. icing sugar

Sift the flour and salt into a mixing bowl, break both eggs into a well in the centre, and stir in half the milk. Mix well, using an electric mixer or a wooden spoon, add the rest of the milk by degrees whisking continuously. Leave the batter to stand for half an hour.

Heat a small frying pan, grease lightly with lard, and when really hot pour in enough batter to cover the bottom of the pan thinly, tilting backwards and forwards to get an even covering. Cook over brisk heat, turn over when brown on one side. If the pancakes are made ahead of time, stack them one above the other with a dusting of sugar between and keep in a cool dry place for a few hours.

Mix the apple purée, sultanas and cinnamon, heat gently and spread this filling over each pancake, then roll up and place on a hot platter. When all the pancakes are done, dust with icing sugar, and keep hot till required. Good with Foamy Custard.

(2) APPLE CHARLOTTE (serves 6 to 8)

170 g (6 oz) fresh white breadcrumbs	1 kg (2 lb) cooking apples
110 g (4 oz) butter or margarine	170 g (6 oz) sugar (or more to taste)

Peel and core the apples, cook with very little water and most of the sugar until soft. Melt the butter, stir in the breadcrumbs lightly with a fork and cook until golden brown. Butter an ovenglass dish and fill with alternate layers of breadcrumbs lightly scattered with sugar, and apple, starting and ending with a layer of breadcrumbs and sugar. Bake in a moderate oven (205° C gas mark 6) for about 30 minutes until brown and crisp on top. Serve with Foamy Custard or cream.

Adjust quantities according to the number of guests, keeping in mind that people usually eat less standing up than they do at table.

Elegant Little Dinner Parties

Four, six or eight are good numbers for a small dinner party. Plan the meal carefully for contrast in taste, texture and colour; if you include a rich main course have a light starter or dessert.

DINNER MENU (1)

Chilled Cheese and Melba Toast (page 57)
Roast Duck (page 80)
New Potatoes with butter and chopped mint (page 113) Sweet Sour Cabbage (page 108) or peas
Hot Pineapple Pudding and cream (Irish soffee) (see below)

HOT PINEAPPLE PUDDING (for 4-6)

430 g (15½ oz) tin pineapple chunks
50 g (2 oz) cornflour
45 g (1½ oz) sugar
For Meringue Topping:
3 rounded tablesp. castor sugar
Reserved pineapple pieces
A little angelica

25 g (1 oz) butter

2 egg yolks
About ½ cup of water

2 egg whites
6 cherries

Drain the juice from the tin into a measuring jug, add water to make the liquid up to 300 ml (½ pint). Melt the butter in a saucepan, add the cornflour and mix to a smooth paste. Pour in the pineapple juice and water slowly, stirring all the while and cook over a low heat until the mixture thickens. Remove from heat, allow to cool a little, and beat in egg yolks and sugar. Add pineapple chunks (reserving 6) and pour into a buttered ovenglass dish.

For Meringue Topping: whisk egg whites until fluffy, fold in the sugar and whisk again until stiff. Spread the meringue mixture over the pudding, raising it into peaks with a fork, and arrange the reserved pineapple chunks, halved cherries and small strips of angelica in a pattern on the top. Bake in a cool oven (145° C gas mark 1) for 30 minutes until the meringue is crisp and golden.

IRISH COFFEE

For each person you need:

One stemmed whiskey glass; very hot, strong black coffee; 1 tablesp. whipped cream; 2 to 3 teasp. sugar; 1 tablesp. Irish Whiskey.

Using a spirit lamp, heat the glass turning carefully so as not to crack it. Heat the whiskey in a tablespoon, pour into the glass, fill with very hot black coffee in which 2 to 3 teaspoons of sugar are dissolved, then float the cream on top. Do not stir. Irish Coffee is ambrosial if really hot, and a criminal waste of whiskey if served lukewarm. Practice beforehand!

DINNER MENU (2) FOR 8 PEOPLE

Savoury Scrambled Egg (recipe following)
Party Chicken and Rice (recipe following)
French Beans
Chocolate Whip (page 74, double quantities)

FOR SAVOURY SCRAMBLED EGG

8 eggs
1 tablesp. chopped parsley
1 dessertsp. chopped chives
4 tablesp. grated cheese
8 small squares of fried bread

2 tomatoes
50 g (2 oz) butter
1 teasp. salt
Pepper

Fry the bread until crisp and golden, drain on kitchen paper and keep hot. The egg mixture may be prepared in advance, it takes five minutes to cook and must be served immediately. Break the eggs into a bowl, beat until yolks and whites are blended, add tomatoes peeled and chopped, parsley and chives (which should be cut into tiny bits with scissors), grated cheese, salt and freshly ground pepper, then mix with a fork. Melt half the butter in a saucepan, pour in the eggs and cook over a medium heat, stirring gently with a metal spoon until the mixture begins to thicken, then add the remaining butter, remove from heat and stir briskly. The eggs should be cooked until soft and creamy, not dry – serve immediately on the fried bread, garnished with a sprig of parsley. A very simple first course, but everyone seems to like it.

PARTY CHICKEN AND RICE

2 roasting chickens (each about
   1½ kg (3 lb)
100 g (4 oz) butter
1 large tin pineapple rings
300 ml (½ pint) chicken stock   or
340 g (12 oz) Patna rice
Salt and pepper

1 large onion
1 lemon
1 heaped tablesp. flour
1 tablesp. milk
a Knorr cube and water
4 tablesp. brandy
2 tablesp. cream

Rub a little of the butter into the chicken skin, sprinkle with salt. Melt the rest of the butter in a roasting pan, add the chopped onion and chickens and cook in a preheated moderately hot oven (205° C gas mark 6) for 15 minutes. Reserve 8 pineapple rings for garnishing, cut the remainder into small pieces and add to the roasting pan with half a cup of the juice, the chicken stock and salt and pepper. Cover the chickens with tinfoil and cook for another 45 minutes or a little longer until tender, basting 3 or 4 times – avoid over-cooking or the chickens will be dry.

Cook the rice in rapidly boiling salted water for 12 to 14 minutes until soft to bite but not mushy, drain through a sieve and hold under the hot tap to separate the grains, dry in the oven for a few minutes. Arrange the rice on a large flat serving dish, place the chickens in the centre, surround with halved pineapple rings, and keep hot – it will not spoil if covered with greaseproof paper in a slow oven.

To make the gravy, mix the flour with the milk, add to the juices in the roasting pan, stir and bring to the boil, add the lemon juice and brandy and boil for 3 minutes. Add the cream and pour the gravy into a sauceboat.

DINNER MENU (3) FOR 6 TO 8 PEOPLE
Cheese Souflé (recipe following)
Cold Ham (page 92) or Cold Chicken (page 77) or Cold Salmon (page 30)

Salad of crisp lettuce, hard boiled eggs, sliced orange, sliced cucumber and tomatoes garnished with chopped chives, with Mayonnaise served separately (page 30)
Potato Salad (page 119)
Chilled Chocolate Cake (recipe following) and ice cream.

CHEESE SOUFFLÉ: (serves 4) MAKE TWO
4 eggs and 1 extra white
Small pinch bread soda (bicarbonate of soda)

250 ml (½ pint) milk
Pinch of Cayenne pepper

170 g (6 oz) grated cheese
1 teasp. mustard
25 g (1 oz) flour
25 g (1 oz) butter
½ teasp. salt

The cheese sauce may be prepared in advance: melt the butter in a saucepan, add the flour and stir over low heat until thickened, add the hot milk slowly, stirring continuously and cook for four minutes until the mixture is smooth and creamy (the hand mixer will remove any lumps). Cool a little, stir in the cheese, mustard, seasoning and egg yolks, leave until ready to make the soufflé, never add the egg whites until the cheese mixture is cool.

Before whipping the egg whites be sure that the oven is preheated to (205° C gas mark 6) moderately hot, and that the soufflé dish is ready: butter the inside of a straight sided 800 ml (1½ pint) ovenproof dish, line the outside with grease-proof paper tied round it. Half an hour before dinner, whip the 5 egg whites with the soda until stiff but not dry, fold gently into the cheese sauce making sure that all is well blended, pour into the prepared dish and place immediately in the oven on a low shelf, bake for 25 minutes, a little longer if you like the consistency dry. Have the guests seated just before the soufflé is due to come out of the oven, – the breadsoda gives it 'lift' for a few extra precious minutes.

Any dry left-overs such as minced ham or flaked cooked fish may be used instead of cheese, use only 110 g (4 oz).

A soufflé is a delicious and impressive start for a meal, to be sure of success reserve the oven, and plan the rest of the menu to fit in with this.

CHILLED CHOCOLATE CAKE (serves 6 to 8)

You need a sponge cake made with:

100 g (4 oz) margarine	100 g (4 oz) castor sugar
100 g (4 oz) self-raising flour	2 eggs
½ teasp. vanilla essence	

For the filling:

100 g (4 oz) plain chocolate	2 tablesp. milk
110 g (4 oz) castor sugar	4 egg yolks
1 teasp. coffee essence	

For topping:

300 ml (½ pint) thick cream	15 g (½ oz) icing sugar
A few cherries and a little angelica	

To make the sponge cake: cream the margarine and sugar until light and fluffy, beat in the eggs and vanilla, fold in the

flour with a metal spoon (to use the hand mixer once the flour
is added makes the cake tough). Grease a rectangular 20 by
30 cm (8 by 12 inch) baking tin, line the bottom with greaseproof paper and spoon the sponge mixture in, smoothing it
and leaving a slight hollow in the centre. Bake in a moderately
hot oven (205° C gas mark 6) for about 10 minutes, it browns
suddenly, so watch carefully. Turn out on a wire rack, strip off
paper and leave to cool.

Line a ½ kg (1 lb) loaf tin with foil, cut the sponge into
narrow fingers and line the bottom of the tin with some of
them. Break the chocolate into pieces and melt it slowly in a
bowl with the milk, over hot water. Whisk the sugar and egg
yolks in another bowl over hot water until creamy and fluffy,
remove from the heat and mix in the chocolate mixture and
the coffee essence. Spoon some of this mixture over the sponge
in the tin. Continue with alternate layers of cake and chocolate
mixture, ending with a layer of cake, put into the refrigerator
and leave for at least 12 hours. Turn out and coat with sweetened whipped cream, garnish with cherries and angelica, and
serve with icecream.

Ideas for a Child's Party

Children seem to have a taste for savoury foods now-a-days:
(1) Small cocktail sausages (or ordinary ones, fried and cut
into short pieces) on sticks, with Tomato Dip (page 47)
(2) Potato Crisps: one packet per child
(3) Sandwiches are popular: buy thin sliced bread and make
small tomato or sardine sandwiches, crusts removed of course –
(bananas mashed with sugar make a good sweet sandwich
filling.)
(4) Swiss Roll Sandwiches: cut all the crusts off a whole fresh
loaf, then cut the bread into long narrow slices length-ways,
instead of downwards as is usual. Spread with softened (not
melted) butter, and a creamy filling such as cold scrambled
eggs with grated cheese and chopped chives, mashed tinned
salmon, or cream cheese mixed with tomato sauce and a little
minced ham. Then roll up from one end like a Swiss roll, press
slightly to make it firm, wrap in foil and put in the refrigerator

for a few hours to set, cut into thin slices – very appetizing.

(5) Rainbow Sandwiches: use a day old loaf, but prepare as above, cutting the crusts off the whole loaf, and slicing into long narrow slices lengthways instead of down, butter all the slices.

Spread cold scrambled egg with chopped chives on the first slice, top with the second slice, butter side down and spread the top of this slice with softened butter, and mashed tinned salmon; then the third slice, butter side down. Spread this with butter, and cream cheese mashed with sardines. Top with the fourth slice, butter side down, and press firmly together. Wrap in foil and leave in the refrigerator to set for a few hours, slice downwards as you would normally cut the loaf, giving a thin sandwich with four layers of bread and three of filling.

(6) Children also like Tiny Scones with Savoury Toppings (page 125), Tiny Sausage Rolls (page 124), and small Savoury Pastries.

Most children also seem to like the following sweet things:

(1) Tiny Meringues (page 132), colour half the mixture pink with a few drops of cochineal, sandwich pink and white meringues together with melted chocolate.

(2) Iced Sponge Buns: make double the sponge mixture given on page 141, put a dessertspoonful of the mixture into each patty tin and bake for about 15 minutes in a moderately hot oven (205° C gas mark 6) until golden brown. Ice with Glacé Icing.

Glacé Icing: crush 220 g (8 oz) icing sugar between two sheets of greaseproof paper with a rolling pin until free of lumps, sieve into a bowl and add 1½ to 2 tablespoons boiling water, beating hard. Ice half of the buns with white icing, colour the remaining icing pink with cochineal, or brown with cocoa, and ice the remaining buns, working rapidly as it sets quickly. Top with a cherry.

(3) Icecream is always popular.

What to Drink?

Cidona, Ribena, orange or lemon squash, fizzy drinks or
home-made lemonade, served in glasses with coloured straws
and ice if possible.

HOME-MADE LEMONADE

340 g (12 oz) sugar   3 lemons
1¾ l (3 pints) water   A few mint leaves

Pare the lemon rinds thinly, simmer with the water, sugar and
mint leaves for five minutes, stirring occasionally. Strain
through a sieve, cool and then add the juice of the lemons, stir
well and serve as cold as possible.

CAKES FOR MORNING COFFEE

Sultana Rock Cakes:

200 g (8 oz) plain flour   6 tablesp. sultanas
50 g (2 oz) margarine   50 g (2 oz) lard
150 g (6 oz) castor sugar   ¼ teasp. salt
1 level teasp. baking powder   1 egg
A little milk

Sift the flour, salt and baking powder, rub in the lard and
margarine until like fine breadcrumbs, add the sugar and
sultanas and mix with the fingers. Add the beaten egg and
about one dessertspoon of milk to make a stiff paste. Using a
fork and spoon place in small pyramids on a greased baking
sheet, and bake in a moderately hot oven (205° C gas mark 6)
for about 14 minutes, turning the baking sheet after 8 minutes.
Nicest when eaten hot.

Walnut and Date Loaf:

100 ml (4 fluid oz) boiling water   100 g (4 oz) dates
25 g (1 oz) chopped walnuts   25 g (1 oz) margarine
100 g (4 oz) self-raising flour   75 g (3 oz) castor sugar
½ teasp. bread soda   1 egg
(bicarbonate of soda)

Sprinkle the chopped dates with the bread soda, pour the boiling water over and leave to get cool. Cream the margarine and sugar, beat in the egg, the date mixture and chopped walnuts. Fold in the sifted flour with a metal spoon, pour the mixture into a greased and lined ½kg (1 lb) loaf tin and bake for an hour in a very moderate oven (180° C gas mark 4) covering if necessary. Cool on a wire rack, serve thinly sliced and buttered.

The Last Word

I once knew a young man – really a most pleasant and well-meaning young man – who, fresh from University, joined a small Irish firm. Within a month he was highly unpopular with the whole staff, most puzzling until I heard an old workman talking about him.

'Sometimes I have pity for him, and more times I haven't', he said. 'There he is, waving his certificates in his hand, proud as a peacock and bursting with judgement.'

What a very apt and telling phrase, I do hope I have not given that impression –! It is just that I believe good food is one of the pleasures and blessings of life; I enjoy cooking, and eating, and talking about food. While writing this book I have discovered so many things that I didn't know before that it has given me a renewed interest in my own kitchen.

I will end as I began with a rather cynical quotation from Owen Meredith:

'He may live without books, – what is knowledge but grieving?
He may live without hope, – what is hope but deceiving?
He may live without love, – what is passion but pining?
But where is the man who can live without dining?'

Index

Does Mrs O'Meara think very much of Kerrygold?

She doesn't have to! Like the 250,000 Irish housewives who use Kerrygold butter, Mrs. O'Meara knows we're doing her Kerrygold thinking for her! Thinking about Kerrygold's creamy goodness. Thinking about Kerrygold's purity. And about making sure that every single pound of Kerrygold reaches her as it leaves us. Dairy fresh. Mrs. O'Meara doesn't have to think too much about Kerrygold. She knows. Kerrygold goodness is a fact of life!